TREKKING IN THE CANARY ISLANDS

About the Author

Paddy Dillon is a prolific walker and guidebook writer, with over 90 guidebooks to his name and contributions to 40 other titles. He has written extensively for many different outdoor publications and has appeared on radio and television.

Paddy uses a tablet computer to write his route descriptions while walking. His descriptions are therefore precise, having been written at the very point at which the reader uses them.

Paddy is an indefatigable long-distance walker who has walked all of Britain's National Trails and several major European trails. He lives on the fringes of the Lake District and has walked, and written about walking, in every county throughout the British Isles. He has led guided walks and walked throughout Europe, as well as in Nepal, Tibet, Korea, Africa and the Rocky Mountains of Canada and the US. Paddy is a member of the Outdoor Writers and Photographers Guild.

Other Cicerone guides by the author

Glyndwr's Way
Mountain Walking in Mallorca
The Cleveland Way and the Yorkshire Wolds Way
The GR5 Trail
The GR20 Corsica
The Great Glen Way
The Irish Coast to Coast Walk
The Mountains of Ireland
The National Trails
The North York Moors
The Pennine Way
The Reivers Way
The South West Coast Path
The Teesdale Way (Martin Collins; updated by Paddy Dillon)
The Wales Coast Path
Trekking in Greenland – the Arctic Circle Trail
Trekking in Mallorca

Trekking in the Alps (contributing author)
Walking and Trekking in Iceland
Walking in County Durham
Walking in Sardinia
Walking in Menorca
Walking in the Azores
Walking in the Isles of Scilly
Walking in the North Pennines
Walking on Arran
Walking on Gran Canaria
Walking on Guernsey
Walking on Jersey
Walking on La Gomera and El Hierro
Walking on Lanzarote and Fuerteventura
Walking on La Palma
Walking on Madeira
Walking on Malta
Walking on Tenerife

TREKKING IN THE CANARY ISLANDS

THE GR131 ISLAND-HOPPING ROUTE

by Paddy Dillon

JUNIPER HOUSE, MURLEY MOSS,
OXENHOLME ROAD, KENDAL, CUMBRIA LA9 7RL
www.cicerone.co.uk

© Paddy Dillon 2020
First edition 2020
ISBN: 978 1 85284 765 4

Printed by KHL Printing, Singapore
A catalogue record for this book is available from the British Library.

Route mapping by Lovell Johns www.lovelljohns.com
All photographs are by the author unless otherwise stated.
Contains OpenStreetMap.org data © OpenStreetMap
contributors, CC-BY-SA. NASA relief data courtesy of ESRI

Updates to this Guide

While every effort is made by our authors to ensure the accuracy of guidebooks as they go to print, changes can occur during the lifetime of an edition. Any updates that we know of for this guide will be on the Cicerone website (www.cicerone.co.uk/908/updates), so please check before planning your trip. We also advise that you check information about such things as transport, accommoda¬tion and shops locally. Even rights of way can be altered over time.

We are always grateful for information about any discrepancies between a guidebook and the facts on the ground, sent by email to updates@cicerone. co.uk or by post to Cicerone, Juniper House, Murley Moss, Oxenholme Road, Kendal, LA9 7RL.

Register your book: To sign up to receive free updates, special offers and GPX files where available, register your book at www.cicerone.co.uk.

Notes on mapping

The route maps in this guide are derived from publicly available data, databases and crowd-sourced data. As such they have not been through the detailed checking procedures that would generally be applied to a published map from an official mapping agency, although naturally we have reviewed them closely in the light of local knowledge as part of the preparation of this guide. The islands are densely forested in places, and there is extensive tree cover which may change over time – although the woodland shown is reasonably representative it should not be considered completely accurate.

Front cover: Degollada de Gujara with El Teide beyond (Stage 23)

CONTENTS

Map key 8
Overview map of the Canary Islands 9
Route summary table 11

INTRODUCTION 15
Location 15
Geology 16
Brief history of the Canary Islands 17
Plants and animals 19
Travel to the Canary Islands 22
Travel around the Canary Islands 23
When to go 26
Accommodation 26
Language 28
Money 29
Food and drink 29
Trekking the GR131 30
Using this guide 30
Emergencies 32

LANZAROTE 33
Stage 1   Órzola to Haría 36
Stage 2   Haría to Teguise 41
Stage 3   Teguise to Montaña Blanca 47
Stage 4   Montaña Blanca to Yaiza 52
Stage 5   Yaiza to Playa Blanca 58

FUERTEVENTURA 63
Stage 6   Islote de Lobos 68
Stage 7   Corralejo to La Oliva 71
Stage 8   La Oliva to Tefía 77
Stage 9   Tefía to Betancuria 83
Stage 10   Betancuria to Pájara 89
Stage 11   Pájara to La Pared 95
Stage 12   La Pared to Barranco de Pecenescal 103
Stage 13   Barranco de Pecenescal to Morro Jable 108
Stage 14   Morro Jable to Faro de Jandía 114

GRAN CANARIA 121
Stage 15   Faro de Maspalomas to Ayagaures. 125
Stage 16   Ayagaures to Tunte 132
Stage 17   Tunte to Cruz de Tejeda. 137
Stage 18   Cruz de Tejeda to Tamadaba 142
Stage 19   Tamadaba to Puerto de las Nieves. 148

TENERIFE 153
Stage 20   La Esperanza to La Caldera 158
Stage 21   La Caldera to El Portillo. 165
Optional route   Ascent of El Teide 171
Stage 22   El Portillo to Parador 179
Stage 23   Parador to Vilaflor 184
Stage 24   Vilaflor to Arona 189

LA GOMERA 195
Stage 25   San Sebastián to Chipude 198
Stage 26   Chipude to Playa de Vallehermoso 206

LA PALMA 213
Stage 27   Faro de Fuencaliente to Fuencaliente 217
Stage 28   Fuencaliente to Refugio El Pilar. 220
Stage 29   Refugio El Pilar to Roque de los Muchachos 226
Stage 30   Roque de los Muchachos to Puerto de Tazacorte. 234

EL HIERRO 241
Stage 31   Puerto de la Estaca or Tamaduste to Fuente de La Llanía 244
Stage 32   Fuente de La Llanía to Embarcadero de Orchilla 252

Appendix A   Language notes. 259
Appendix B   Useful contacts. 262

Mountain safety

Every mountain walk has its dangers, and those described in this guidebook are no exception. All who walk or climb in the mountains should recognise this and take responsibility for themselves and their companions along the way. The author and publisher have made every effort to ensure that the information contained in this guide was correct when it went to press, but, except for any liability that cannot be excluded by law, they cannot accept responsibility for any loss, injury or inconvenience sustained by any person using this book.

International distress signal *(emergency only)*
Six blasts on a whistle (and flashes with a torch after dark) spaced evenly for one minute, followed by a minute's pause. Repeat until an answer is received. The response is three signals per minute followed by a minute's pause.

Helicopter rescue
The following signals are used to communicate with a helicopter:

Help needed:
raise both arms
above head to
form a 'Y'

Help not needed:
raise one arm
above head, extend
other arm downward

Emergency telephone numbers
International emergency number: 112
Guardia Civil: 062

Mountain rescue can be very expensive – be adequately insured.

Symbols used on route maps

～	route
～	alternative route
⁄‒‒	track
⁄‒‒	footpath
(S)	start point
(F)	finish point
(SF)	start/finish point
(S)	alternative start point
(F)	alternative finish point
➤	route direction
	woodland
	urban areas
	marshland
▲	peak
•	other feature
■	building
⛴	ferry
⊕	airport

Relief
in metres

3800–4000	
3600–3800	
3400–3600	
3200–3400	
3000–3200	
2800–3000	
2600–2800	
2400–2600	
2200–2400	
2000–2200	
1800–2000	
1600–1800	
1400–1600	
1200–1400	
1000–1200	
800–1000	
600–800	
400–600	
200–400	
0–200	

SCALE: 1:50,000

0 kilometres	0.5	1
0 miles		0.5

GPX files for all routes can be downloaded free at www.cicerone.co.uk/765/GPX.

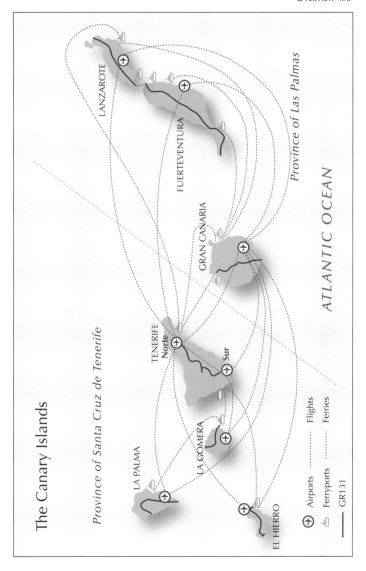

The Canary Islands

Province of Santa Cruz de Tenerife

Province of Las Palmas

ATLANTIC OCEAN

LANZAROTE

FUERTEVENTURA

GRAN CANARIA

TENERIFE
Norte
Sur

LA PALMA

LA GOMERA

EL HIERRO

⊕ Airports
⚓ Ferryports
— GR131

Flights ·········
Ferries ·········

Rock overhangs a splendid paved path high above Cruz Grande (Stage 17)

ROUTE SUMMARY TABLE

Stage no	Start	Distance	Time	Ascent	Descent
Lanzarote					
Stage 1	Órzola	12km (7½ miles)	3hr 30min	470m (1540ft)	190m (625ft)
Stage 2	Haría	13km (8 miles)	4hr 30min	360m (1180ft)	340m (1115ft)
Stage 3	Teguise	15.5km (9¾ miles)	4hr 30min	270m (885ft)	300m (985ft)
Stage 4	Montaña Blanca	17km (10½ miles)	5hr	390m (1280ft)	480m (1575ft)
Stage 5	Yaiza	15.5km (9¾ miles)	5hr	80m (260ft)	260m (855ft)
Lanzarote total		73km (45¼ miles)	5 days	1570m (5150ft)	1570m (5150ft)
Fuerteventura					
Stage 6	Islote de Lobos	8km (5 miles)	2hr 30min	150m (490ft)	150m (490ft)
Stage 7	Corralejo	25km (15½ miles)	8hr	480m (1575ft)	260m (855ft)
Stage 8	La Oliva	17.5km (11 miles)	5hr 30min	210m (690ft)	230m (755ft)
Stage 9	Tefía	17.5km (11 miles)	6hr	530m (1740ft)	340m (1115ft)
Stage 10	Betancuria	17km (10½ miles)	5hr 30min	520m (1705ft)	710m (2330ft)
Stage 11	Pájara	26km (16 miles)	9hr	750m (2460ft)	910m (2985ft)
Stage 12	La Pared	16km (10 miles)	5hr	290m (950ft)	280m (920ft)
Stage 13	Barranco de Pecenescal	16.5km (10¼ miles)	5hr	400m (1315ft)	450m (1475ft)
Stage 14	Morro Jable	20.5km (12¾ miles)	6hr	280m (920ft)	280m (920ft)
Fuerteventura total		164km (102 miles)	9 days	3610m (11,845ft)	3610m (11,845ft)

Stage no	Start	Distance	Time	Ascent	Descent
Gran Canaria					
Stage 15	Faro de Maspalomas	18km (11¼ miles)	5hr 30min	530m (1740ft)	220m (720ft)
Stage 16	Ayagaures	12.5km (7¾ miles)	4hr	900m (2950ft)	320m (1050ft)
Stage 17	Tunte	15.5km (9½ miles)	5hr 30min	1020m (3345ft)	400m (1310ft)
Stage 18	Cruz de Tejeda	17.5km (11 miles)	5hr 30min	750m (2460ft)	1060m (3475ft)
Stage 19	Tamadaba	10.5km (6½ miles)	3hr 30min	50m (165ft)	1250m (4100ft)
Gran Canaria total		74km (46 miles)	5 days	3250m (10,660ft)	3250m (10,660ft)
Tenerife					
Stage 20	La Esperanza	29.5km (18¼ miles)	10hr	1650m (5415ft)	1360m (4460ft)
Stage 21	La Caldera	13.5km (8¼ miles)	5hr	1090m (3575ft)	240m (790ft)
Teide Alt 1	El Portillo	11.5km (7 miles)	5hr	1250m (4100ft)	20m (65ft)
Teide Alt 2	Refugio Alta Vista	13km (8 miles)	5hr	450m (1475ft)	1570m (5150ft)
Stage 22	El Portillo	17km (10½ miles)	5hr	260m (855ft)	150m (490ft)
Stage 23	Parador	15.5km (9¾ miles)	5hr 30min	380m (1245ft)	1100m (3610ft)
Stage 24	Vilaflor	18km (11 miles)	6hr	450m (1475ft)	1260m (4135ft)
Tenerife total		93.5km (58 miles)	5 days	3830m (12,565ft)	4110m (13,485ft)
Tenerife total (El Teide alternative)		101km (62¾ miles)	6 days	5270m (17,290ft)	5550m (18,210ft)

Stage no	Start	Distance	Time	Ascent	Descent
La Gomera					
Stage 25	San Sebastián	27km (16¾ miles)	10hr	1960m (6430ft)	880m (2885ft)
Stage 26	Chipude	18.5km (11½ miles)	6hr	420m (1380ft)	1500m (4920ft)
La Gomera total		45.5km (28¼ miles)	2 days	2380m (7810ft))	2380m (7810ft)
La Palma					
Stage 27	Faro de Fuencaliente	7km (4¼ miles)	2hr 30min	710m (2330ft)	0m (0ft)
Stage 28	Fuencaliente	17.5km (10¾ miles)	6hr	1450m (4760ft)	720m (2360ft)
Stage 29	Refugio El Pilar	27km (16¾ miles)	9hr	1880m (6170ft)	900m (2950ft)
Stage 30	Roque de los Muchachos	18km (11 miles)	5hr 30min	100m (330ft)	2520m (8270ft)
La Palma total		69.5km (43¼ miles)	4 days	4140m (13,585ft)	4140m (13,585ft)
El Hierro					
Stage 31	Puerto de la Estaca/ Tamaduste	18km (11 miles)	5hr 30min	1440m (4725ft)	100m (330ft)
Stage 32	Fuente de La Llanía	22km (14 miles)	7hr	240m (790ft)	1580m (5185ft)
El Hierro total		40km (25 miles)	2 days	1680m (5510ft)	1680m (5510ft)
GR131 total		559.5km (347½ miles)	32 days	20,460m (67,125ft)	20,740m (68,045ft)
GR131 total (El Teide alternative)		567km (352 miles)	33 days	21,900m (71,850ft)	22,180m (72,770ft)

Climbing past terraces in the Valle de Malpaso above Haría (Stage 2)

INTRODUCTION

The Canary Islands comprise seven subtropical islands with enviable weather and a great variety of scenery. Who wouldn't want to trek all the way across them, one after another? There are rugged coastlines and occasional sandy beaches, arid slopes of aromatic scrub, steep and rugged mountains clothed in extensive pine forests and curious laurisilva 'cloud forests', with the possibility of snow-capped peaks rising even higher in the winter months. The GR131 is an island-hopping trail that runs coast to coast across each of the islands in turn and often seeks out the highest mountains during each traverse. It measures 560km (348 miles) and would take an average trekker about one month to complete.

The GR131 is described from east to west, starting on the arid, volcanic island of Lanzarote, later taking a short ferry ride to the desert-like Fuerteventura. A long ferry ride leads to Gran Canaria, where the mountains rise higher and feature extensive forests. Another ferry ride leads to Tenerife, where the GR131 stays high, featuring more forests, with even more rugged mountains rising above them. An option is presented to vary the route and include the mighty El Teide – the highest mountain on Spanish territory. A short ferry ride to La Gomera sees the trail climb high into extensive laurisilva 'cloud forest'. A longer ferry ride leads to La Palma, where the trail climbs high and stays on the highest mountains, offering a particularly tough traverse ending with a steep descent. The GR131 finally finds itself making a high-level traverse through the smallest and westernmost island of El Hierro, ending at a point that was once believed to be the edge of the world.

The GR131 deserves to be one of the classic treks of the world, but because of its fragmented nature and the fact that it has been pieced together over several years, many trekkers aren't even aware of its existence. The signposting and waymarking of the trail is largely consistent across the islands, so there is a fine sense of continuity, despite the frequent breaks while catching ferries from island to island. It is often possible to see the next island ahead, maybe with its highest mountains poking through a 'sea of clouds' that often forms around them. There is always something to look forward to, and something to look back at, on a journey such as this one.

LOCATION

The Canary Islands are more or less enclosed in a rectangular area from 13°30'W to 18°00'W and 27°30'N to 29°30'N. As a group, they stretch from east to west over 450km (280 miles). Although administered by Spain, the mother country is 1100km (685 miles)

Gran Canaria's intricate valleys as seen from Monte Constantino (Stage 19)

away. The narrowest strait between the Canary Islands and Africa is a mere 110km (70 miles). The total land area is almost 7500km² (2900 square miles), but the area of sea they occupy is 10 times that size.

GEOLOGY

Most of the world's volcanic landscapes are formed where huge continental or oceanic 'plates' collide with each other or tear apart. When continental plates collide the Earth's crust crumples upwards to form mountains, and when plates are torn apart, basaltic lava from deep with the Earth's mantle erupts as volcanoes. The Canary Islands, however, are different and have a more complicated geological history.

The African landmass is the visible part of a continental plate that extends into the Atlantic Ocean, while the Canary Islands lie within the oceanic crust of the eastern Atlantic Ocean, close to the passive junction with the African continental plate. It is thought that the islands lie directly above a hot-spot, or mantle plume, some 2500km (1550 miles) deep within the Earth. The mantle plume is fixed, but the oceanic and African plates are drifting very slowly eastwards. Every so often a split in the oceanic crust opens above the mantle plume, allowing molten rock to vent onto the ocean floor. As more and more material erupts, it piles higher and higher until it rises from the sea. Each of the Canary Islands was formed in this way.

Lanzarote and Fuerteventura, the first Canary Islands to form, were subsequently pulled eastwards. The next time a rift opened over the mantle plume the islands of Gran Canaria and Tenerife were formed, and these too were pulled eastwards. A further oceanic rift led to the formation of La Gomera, La Palma and El Hierro. Looking forward in geological time more islands are bound to appear as other rifts are torn open in the future. In fact, a minor undersea eruption took place off the coast of El Hierro between October 2011 and March 2012, so the process is clearly ongoing.

The forces at work deep within the Earth can scarcely be imagined. Every single piece of rock in the Canary Islands once existed in a molten state. Consider the energy needed to melt one small stone, and multiply that to imagine the energy required to melt everything in the island chain, as well as the immense amount of rock beneath the sea that supports them all!

Over time huge amounts of volcanic material were piled high, but some of it was inherently unstable. During recent geological time vast chunks of the islands have collapsed into the sea, creating features such as the Orotava valley on Tenerife, the Caldera de Taburiente on La Palma and El Golfo on El Hierro. With each catastrophic collapse tsunamis were generated, which devastated places around the Atlantic Ocean. Geologists predict that similar collapses could take place in future on the north face of El Teide on Tenerife, or on the Cumbre Nueva on La Palma.

The Canary Islands are volcanic and this is an example of ropy lava

BRIEF HISTORY OF THE CANARY ISLANDS

Myths and legends speak of 'The Fortunate Isles', or 'Isles of the Blessed', lying somewhere in the Atlantic, enjoying a wonderful climate and bearing all manner of fruit. The rebel Roman general Sertorius planned to retire there, while Plutarch referred to them many times, though Pliny warned 'these islands, however, are greatly annoyed by the bodies of monsters, which are constantly thrown up by the sea.' Maybe these scribes knew of the Canary Islands, or maybe they

17

were drawing on older Phoenician or Carthaginian references. Some would even claim that the islands were the last remnants of Atlantis.

The original inhabitants were often described as a 'stone-age' culture and are thought to have arrived from the Berber areas of North Africa well over 2000 years ago. They are generally referred to as 'Guanches', though this is really the term for the aboriginals of Tenerife. In Lanzarote and Fuerteventura they were the Majoreros. In Gran Canaria they were the Canarians. In La Gomera they were the Gomeritas. In La Palma they were the Benahoares. In El Hierro they were the Bimbaches. Although technologically primitive, their society was well ordered and they had a special regard for monumental rock forms, caves and other natural features.

The inhabitants fiercely resisted the well-armed Spaniards during the 15th century Conquest of the islands, but one by one each island fell. Tenerife capitulated last of all, with the mighty volcano of El Teide grumbling throughout. Many aboriginals were slaughtered or enslaved, but some entered into treaties, converted to Christianity and intermarried with the invaders. Though the natives lost their land and freedom, their blood flows in the veins of modern Canarios and vestiges of their traditions live on, as do some of their place names.

The Canary Islands were visited by Christopher Columbus on his voyage of discovery in 1492. Subsequently,

Statues of the aboriginal chiefs of Fuerteventura (Stage 9)

the islands were used as stepping stones to the Americas, and many Canarios emigrated. The islands were exposed and, as they weren't always defended with military might, they were subject to pirate raids, endured disputes with the Portuguese, were attacked by the British and suffered wavering economic fortunes.

There was constant rivalry between Tenerife and Gran Canaria, with the entire island group being governed from Las Palmas de Gran Canaria from 1808, before Santa Cruz de Tenerife became the capital in 1822. In 1927 the Canary Islands were divided into two provinces, with Las Palmas encompassing the three eastern islands and Santa Cruz de Tenerife encompassing the four western islands.

In the early 20th century the military governor of the Canary Islands, General Franco, departed for North Africa to launch a military coup. This marked the onset of the infamous Civil War, leading to the creation of the Spanish Republic, followed by a long and repressive dictatorship. The Canary Islands remained free of the worst strife of the Civil War, but also became something of a backwater. It was largely as a result of Franco's later policies that the Canary Islands were developed in the 1960s as a major destination for northern Europeans.

Since 1982 the islands have been an autonomous region and there have been calls for complete independence from Spain. The islanders regard themselves as 'Canarios' first and 'Spanish' second, though they are also fiercely loyal to their own particular islands, towns and villages. Good-quality signposted and waymarked trails, including the development of the GR131, date from an initiative launched on La Palma in 1999, endorsed by the European Ramblers' Association.

PLANTS AND ANIMALS

The Canary Islands are geologically young and when they emerged from the ocean as molten lava and volcanic ash they were quite sterile. In time they were colonised by plants, arriving as windblown seeds and spores, or as seeds washed up from the sea. Birds and insects had no problem landing on the islands before

colonising them. While the northern hemisphere was in the grip of an Ice Age, the Canary Islands were sluiced by rainstorms, with powerful rivers carving deep, steep-sided barrancos into unstable layers of lava and ash. When the land was so well watered it would have borne a particular assemblage of plants, then when the islands later became considerably drier, the range of plants adapted to cope with minimal water.

Trees

Canary pines flourish on high, dry mountainsides, sometimes in places where nothing else grows. Almost every pine you see will have a blackened, scorched trunk, but they regenerate surprisingly well after forest fires. Beware of thick mats of long pine needles on the ground, as they are slippery underfoot. Canary palms also flourish in dry places at lower altitudes, and in the past every part of the tree had a use. Today they provide delicious *miel de palma*, or palm syrup. Every so often dragon trees occur, the last surviving descendants of ancient prehistoric forests. They have been decimated in the wild but prove popular in gardens.

Tagasaste trees are sometimes found in dense plantations, always in places where livestock are grazed. They grow with little water, yet have a high nutritional content and are regularly cut for animal fodder. In recent years they have been exported to Australia. Junipers are common on

Laurisilva 'cloud forest' is found on most of the Canary Islands

some dry slopes. Fruit and nut trees have been established, including apples, oranges, lemons, bananas, almonds, figs and vines. Prickly pears are abundant and their fruit can be harvested, but they were originally introduced for raising cochineal beetles, whose bodies provide a vivid red dye.

On the higher parts of many of the Canary Islands, laurisilva 'cloud forests' are able to trap moisture from the mists and keep themselves well-watered. These forests once spread all the way round the Mediterranean and tropical regions but are now very limited in extent. The laurisilva forest covering the uplands of La Gomera, protected within a national park, is one of the best remaining in the world.

Flowers

Bushy scrub is rich and varied around the Canary Islands, including sticky-leaved cistus and a host of species that walkers should learn to identify. These include bushy, rubbery *tabaibal*, and tall *cardón*, or candelabra spurge. Both have milky latex sap, as does tangled *cornical*, that creeps over the ground and drystone walls, and *aulaga*, which looks like tangled masses of spines often found colonising old cultivation terraces in arid areas. Aromatic, pale green *incienso* is a bushy plant that, with *salado*, grows densely on many of the arid lower slopes of the islands. Fragrant lavender and rosemary usually grow in arid, rocky or stony areas among other scrub species. Of particular importance on Gran Canaria are bushy white *tajinaste*, and the rarer blue _tajinaste_, which grows only on the island. Giant _tajinaste_ grow on the mountains of Tenerife and La Palma. Few of the plants have common English names, but all of them feature so often that they should be learned. Some plants have such limited ranges that the only specimens you are likely to see in the entire world occur on specific stretches of the GR131.

Flowers grow all year round, but visitors in spring and early summer will be amazed at the colour and wealth of flowering plants. Many are Canarian endemics and even trying to compile a shortlist would be pointless. Anyone with a particular interest in flowers and other plants should carry a field guide, in English. Try _Native Flora of the Canary Islands_, by Miguel Ángel Cabrera Pérez, Editorial Everest, or _Wild Flowers of the Canary Islands_, by David Bramwell and Zoë Bramwell, Editorial Rueda.

Animals

As befits remote islands created in relatively recent geological time, the main animal groups to colonise the land were winged creatures, insects and birds. The largest indigenous land mammals were bats. Large and small lizards also arrived, possibly clinging to driftwood. The laurisilva 'cloud forest' is home to the laurel pigeon, while the rock pigeon prefers cliffs. Buzzards and kestrels can be spotted hunting, while ospreys are struggling. Ravens and choughs are common in some places. There are several varieties of pipit, chaffinch, warbler and chiffchaff. One of the smallest birds is the kinglet, a relative of the goldcrest. There are canaries, which have nothing to do with the name of the islands, and parakeets add a flash of colour. The islands attract plenty of passage migrants, and there are escapees from aviaries. The coastal fringes are colonised by gulls, while shearwaters and storm petrels spend most of their time on open water, far from land.

Once the Guanche people arrived and colonised the islands over 2000 ago, the forests suffered as much from clearance as from grazing by voracious goats. Following the Conquest in the 15th century, the Spanish brought in other domestic animals. Cats had a particularly devastating impact on the native wildlife, practically wiping out the giant Canarian lizards, which have only recently been rescued from the edge of extinction on El Hierro. The largest lizards on Gran Canaria survived near Las Palmas simply because they were adopted as pets! Rabbits chew their way through the vegetation and appear regularly on Canarian menus.

There are occasional oddities. Ground squirrels were released in Fuerteventura and can sometimes be seen in great numbers, but they aren't found on any of the other islands. The sea is frequented by whales and dolphins, best seen by taking a specific whale- or dolphin-watching boat trip, though that involves leaving the GR131 entirely.

Protected areas

The Canary Islands feature a handful of national parks and many other protected areas. There are national parks on Lanzarote, Tenerife, La Gomera and La Palma. Most of the islands have been entirely designated as Biosphere Reserves, though only parts of Gran Canaria and Tenerife have been designated. Large parts of all the islands have been protected in other ways, such as Parque Rural (Rural Park), Parque Natural (Natural Park), Paisaje Protegido (Protected Land), Reserva Natural Especial (Special Nature Reserve), Monumento Natural (Natural Monument), and so on. Prominent notices along the course of the GR131 tell walkers when they are entering or leaving these areas, and in fact the bulk of the route runs through a variety of protected areas. There are occasional visitor centres where more information can be studied and where interesting literature can be obtained.

TRAVEL TO THE CANARY ISLANDS

Flights

The vast majority of travellers fly to the Canary Islands and there is a bewildering choice of departure airports from all parts of Britain and Europe, as well as a few flights from the USA. There are several airlines to choose between, including national carriers and budget options. Flight prices vary enormously so if you have any flexibility with the dates for your trip, then search online to find the best deals. Choosing appropriate flights depends largely on how you plan to structure your trip.

Information boards offer background information

If you are planning to walk the entire GR131, then the best approach is to book a flight to Lanzarote and start walking. It will take at least a month to complete the trek, so at some point when the final parts of the schedule fall into place, it is worth checking the availability of flights home. Given that the trek ends on El Hierro, the quickest exit might well involve a flight off the island, so there will be a choice of landing on Tenerife or Gran Canaria. If landing on Tenerife, it might be necessary to switch from the domestic Tenerife Nord airport to the international Tenerife Sur airport. If flying from El Hierro to Gran Canaria, then the homeward flight can be arranged from there. If booking a return flight before even leaving home, then you need to be absolutely sure that you are going to be able to stick to your trekking plan and finish in time to catch the homeward flight.

If the GR131 is to be covered one or two islands at a time, then the outward and return flights could be arranged from other islands. Lanzarote, Fuerteventura, Gran Canaria and Tenerife are all served by a number of airlines from several countries. La Palma is served by very few international flights. La Gomera and El Hierro are served only by domestic inter-island flights.

TRAVEL AROUND THE CANARY ISLANDS

Flights

There are short, fast and frequent flights between some adjacent islands, but not all of them. For instance, there are no

The GR131 begins with an easy road-walk inland from Órzola (Stage 1)

23

direct flights between Lanzarote and Fuerteventura, which is presumably because there are fast and frequent ferries covering the short distance between the islands, and it certainly makes more sense for trekkers to go by boat, rather than fly. Nor are there direct flights between the small western islands of La Gomera, La Palma and El Hierro. Flying between these islands always involves a connection in Tenerife. When there are large distances between the islands, where ferries might only run once or twice a day, maybe even skipping a day, then the notion of taking a flight begins to appeal. The main operators are Binter Canarias, tel 902 391 392 www.bintercanarias. com, and Canaryfly, tel 928 018 500 www.canaryfly.es.

Please note that while flights between the islands may be short, you need to allow plenty of time for check-in and security procedures. It is also necessary to produce a valid passport or national identity card in order to board an aircraft. Also note that there are concessionary discounts on inter-island routes, if you qualify for them.

Ferries

Some stretches of the GR131 start or finish very conveniently at ferry-ports. Even when this isn't the case there are usually good bus services between the trail and ferry-ports. There are two main ferry operators linking the Canary Islands and you can usually choose between them each time you move

All seven of the Canary Islands are linked by ferry services

from island to island. Fred Olsen, tel 902 100 107 www.fredolsen.es, generally operates fast sailings, but at a high price. Naviera Armas, tel 902 456 500 www.navieraarmas.com, generally operates slower sailings, but at a lower price. At the time of writing, only Fred Olsen links Puerto de las Nieves on Gran Canaria with Santa Cruz on Tenerife, and only Naviera Armas links Los Cristianos on Tenerife with Puerto de la Estaca on El Hierro. Depending on how you structure your ferry connections along the GR131, it could take a minimum of nine separate ferries to achieve all the links in the trail, totalling 700km (435m miles) of sailing. That is more than the length of the GR131.

Please note that while ferry tickets can be booked online, or bought on arrival at the ferry-ports, you must produce a valid passport or national identity card in order to board a ferry.

A remote bus stop at the end of the Jandía peninsula (Stage 14)

Also note that there are concessionary discounts available on the ferries, if you qualify for them.

Buses

From time to time it will be necessary to catch one or more buses to reach the start of a stretch of the GR131, or to leave it when transferring to the next stretch. Buses might also be used to 'commute' to and from particular stretches of the trail; this often appeals on those parts that lack nearby accommodation. Each island is served by its own bus company – Lanzarote (Intercity Bus), Fuerteventura (Tiadhe), Gran Canaria (Global), Tenerife (TITSA), La Gomera (GuaguaGomera), La Palma (TILP) and El Hierro (TransHierro). See Appendix B for contact details. Sometimes, the bus services can be remarkably useful, but even so, some of the most useful routes may only run once or twice

a day, in which case you must take great care to be on time if planning to use them. Occasionally, another bus service might be available, but in some cases the only way to get to or from a particular stretch of the GR131 will involve hiring a taxi.

There are usually two ways to pay for bus travel. If using cash, it is best to have a handful of loose change available and don't expect the bus driver to deal with anything larger than a €10 note. Many bus companies issue cards, usually known as 'bonos', that can be pre-charged with an amount of cash. Although these *bonos* offer significant discounts on fares, trekkers who will be walking most of the time and only rarely using buses will probably find it best to use cash.

Vehicle backup

If vehicle backup is to be considered, then vehicles can be hired on each island in turn. Most car hire firms insist that cars hired on one island remain on that island. Even if the hire firm allows cars to be taken from island to island, this usually involves considerable additional expense. Choose a driver who is a good navigator, because they might need to meet you where the GR131 crosses a remote and unfrequented country road, and there might not be space to park beside some roads. Note that one of the places where a pick-up and drop-off might be advantageous, on the summit of Roque de los Muchachos on La Palma, the road cannot be used at night. Several firms offer car hire, including Avis, Cicar, Europcar and Goldcar. The best places to find their offices are at the airports and always be sure to understand the hire regulations.

WHEN TO GO

Spring is often an excellent time to explore the Canary Islands and trek along the GR131. The ground has generally been moistened through the winter, so that fresh green growth and an abundance of flowers can be enjoyed. March and April are likely to the best, but February and May could also be good. It might be best to avoid the peak summer months, because it does get rather too hot for strenuous walking, and towards the end of summer everything begins to look scorched and hazy. However, there can be good weather at any time of the year in the Canary Islands, even through autumn and into winter, but there is a chance that it will be wetter and cooler, even becoming cold with prolonged periods of cloud cover on the mountains. The very highest parts of the GR131, through the Cañadas del Teide on Tenerife, or over the Roque de los Muchachos on La Palma, get snow cover in the winter. When the snow is subject to a period of freeze/thaw and it turns to ice, it can be too dangerous to walk some stretches of mountain paths, though this is only rarely a problem. Road access to those places can be closed temporarily when it snows,

but the moment the roads re-open it is surprising how many Canarios turn up with skis, snowboards and toboggans.

Although the weather is usually very good for walking, bad weather can occur at any time and on rare occasions it can be severe. It is always worth checking the weather forecast. The Weather Channel, www.weather.com, is designed to report the weather for specific locations, offering anything from an hourly to a 10-day forecast. Local newspapers are usually left lying on tables in bars and cafés, and it is always worth having a glance at the weather forecast pages, which are easily understood.

ACCOMMODATION

The Canary Islands offer abundant accommodation options, but the vast majority of them are inappropriate for trekkers on the GR131, either because they lie too far off-route, or because they are just the wrong type of accommodation for those who are constantly on the move. The best way to arrange accommodation is by using online services such as Airbnb, www.airbnb.com, Booking. com, www.booking.com, or any other popular online system. The advantage of using these is that you can usually make bookings at short notice and be able to see a choice of properties in the areas where you want to stay. On a trek as long as the GR131, where all sorts of things

Snow is rare, but it can snow on the highest mountains in winter

could alter your schedule, it isn't wise to book all your overnights a long time in advance. One delayed flight, missed bus or cancelled ferry, and there is a risk that all your advance arrangements could fall apart. The effort involved in re-booking everything at the last minute would be time-consuming and stressful. Booking one, two or three nights in advance is usually the best way to go. You also need to decide whether to operate from a number of bases, moving on every few days, or try to stay on or near the trail each night. A number of specific accommodation options are mentioned in the route descriptions, particularly when the choice is limited. However, these are for information only, and are not intended as recommendations.

Several trekkers have successfully camped along the GR131, but it has to be said at the outset that there are barely a handful of very basic campsites along the entire trail, and while these are usually free of charge, you are expected to apply for permits to use them, which can be time-consuming, bureaucratic and awkward if you have to leave the trail to collect a permit in person from a distant municipal office. Wild camping is illegal, but trekkers have managed to find themselves discreet pitches, drawn no attention to their occupancy and left their pitches absolutely spotless on leaving, with no harm done. The only places where specific penalties are spelled out in law occur on the coast, where the Ley de Costas (Law of the Coast) applies. Apparently, wild camping attracts a fine of €40 per square metre occupied per night, which, in the case of a small tent, might amount to €100, provided

A simple trail shelter and picnic table in Fuerteventura (Stage 10)

that you got 'caught' by someone with authority to apply such a fine. The author has never been caught and has never met anyone who has been caught wild camping.

A number of very basic trail shelters have been constructed across Fuerteventura, and there are a few open shelters along the trail on other islands, usually at large picnic sites. Although they are designed to shelter picnickers, they have occasionally been used as overnight shelters by trekkers. There is a basic refuge high in the mountains on La Palma that could prove useful. Details of any shelters along the way are given in the route description.

LANGUAGE

Castilian Spanish is spoken throughout the Canary Islands, though in most resorts and large hotels there are plenty of English and German speakers. Those who travel through remote rural parts will need at least a few basic phrases of Spanish. Anyone with any proficiency in Spanish will quickly realise that the Canarios have their own accent and colloquialisms. For instance, the letter 's' often vanishes from the middle or end of words, to be replaced by a gentle 'h', or even a completely soundless gap. 'Los Cristianos', for example, becomes 'Loh Cri-tiano'. A bus is referred to as an *autobús* in Spain, but as a *guagua* throughout the Canary Islands. Some natives may seize the opportunity to practise their English with you, while others may be puzzled by your command of Spanish. No matter how bad you think you sound, you will not be the worst they've heard! See Appendix A for placename translations.

Looking from El Muelle on the Islote de Lobos across to Corralejo (Stage 6)

MONEY

The Euro is the currency of the Canary Islands. Large denomination Euro notes are difficult to use for small purchases, so avoid the €500 and €200 notes altogether, and avoid the €100 notes if you can. The rest are fine: €50, €20, €10 and €5. Coins come in €2 and €1. Small denomination coins come in values of 50c, 20c, 10c, 5c, 2c and 1c. Banks and ATMs are mentioned where they occur, in case cash is needed. Many accommodation providers accept major credit and debit cards, as will large supermarkets, but small bars, shops and cafés deal only in cash.

FOOD AND DRINK

All the towns along the GR131 offer shops, bars and restaurants. Most of the villages offer at least a bar-restaurant and possibly a small shop. However, some villages have nothing to offer passing walkers, or their little bar and shop might be closed on arrival. It is always a good idea to carry enough food and water to last until there is an opportunity to restock, and it is wise to carry a little extra just in case it's not possible to restock. There are stretches of the GR131 where food and drink can be bought at the start, in the middle, and at the end of some daily stages. There are other stretches where it might not be possible to buy anything for two or three days. The route description will indicate whether food and drink are available along the way.

If you are walking the GR131 and using public transport to join and leave the route, then no doubt you will be operating from a number of bases where food and drink are readily available. If you are backpacking and wild camping, then it is likely that at times you will need to stock up with plenty of food to cover for those stages where nothing is available, and it will be necessary to obtain water wherever possible, even if that means knocking on someone's door and begging for a bottle to be filled.

If eating in cafés, bars or restaurants, then it is likely that Canarian dishes will be on the menu. Sometimes, food may be on display in glass-fronted cabinets and a selection can be obtained simply by pointing to things. At other times there might be an extensive menu, listing familiar and unfamiliar items. Goat's cheese abounds on the islands and makes its way into many dishes. *Papas arrugadas* are small, wrinkly potatoes baked in salt, dipped in hot *mojo rojo* sauce or the gentler *mojo verde*. Odd as it might sound, these things make a splendid snack in hot weather. Many fish dishes are based on *vieja* and, while all kinds of meat might be available, goat and rabbit are popular. If stews or soups are ordered, they might be accompanied by a pot of *gofio*, which is toasted flour, and the idea is to sprinkle it over the dish and mix it in to achieve a thicker texture.

where the island authorities have for some reason neglected to define their stretch of the GR131. However, there are other popular and well-signposted routes that offer the same level of experience as on the other islands, providing a coast-to-coast route and a high-level traverse. On all the islands, there are centuries-old trails that were popular long before they were incorporated into the GR131, but there are also stretches of the route that have been specifically created and aren't yet popular, where it is possible to stride most of the way through the day without meeting anyone. For the time being, it will be unusual for anyone trekking the whole of the GR131 to meet more than one or two other trekkers following the entire trail, though that is bound to change as the route becomes better known. It really deserves to become one of the world's classic trails.

It is worth bearing in mind that the GR131 is an integral part of the trans-European E7 route, which is currently very fragmented, though in time it is planned to stretch over 6000km (3730 miles) from the Black Sea to El Hierro.

TREKKING THE GR131

A standard form of signposts and waymarks is used throughout the GR131, so there is a sense of continuity from island to island. The exception is on Gran Canaria,

USING THIS GUIDE

This guidebook assumes that trekkers will start their journey at Órzola on Lanzarote. The assumption is also made that they will follow the trail across the Canary Islands in the following order from east to west – Lanzarote, Fuerteventura, Gran Canaria, Tenerife, La Gomera, La Palma and El Hierro. The end of the GR131 will therefore be at the Embarcadero de Orchilla, in a very remote part of El Hierro, once regarded as the edge of the known world. So, the GR131 is a trail to the edge of the world!

Given the direction of travel and the order in which the islands are traversed, the route descriptions on each island have a specific start and finish point. There are also specific ferry journeys linking the islands, and specific bus routes that allow different parts of the trail to be accessed. In short, everything

Standard GR131 marker post; signpost and map-board

appears in a logical order from start to finish. However, there is nothing to stop you customising the route in any way you feel is appropriate, or even reversing the entire route. Instead of trekking for a month, you might make several visits lasting only a week or so, or maybe just visit one island at a time over a period of years. A few short detours are mentioned, but the only major optional detour involves climbing to the summit of El Teide on Tenerife. This is the highest mountain on Spanish territory and as an ascent can be incorporated into the trail; full details are given.

On each island, and along each daily stage of the GR131, notes explain whether there are shops, bar-restaurants or other services available. It is always wise to carry some food and water, just in case places along the way are closed, and always take note of long stretches where there are no opportunities to obtain food and drink. Very occasionally, it might be difficult to join or leave a stretch of the trail, and at those points these difficulties are mentioned so that solutions can be found in good time.

The information box at the beginning of each stage provides the essential statistics for the day's walk: start and finish points, distance covered, total ascent and descent, the length of time it's likely to take to complete the stage, the terrain you will encounter, and places en route where you can buy refreshments. Buses are mentioned wherever they operate, as is any accommodation that is available for that stage.

GPX files

GPX tracks for the routes in this guidebook are available to download free at www.cicerone.co.uk/765/GPX. A GPS device is an excellent aid to navigation, but you should also carry a map and compass and know how to use them. GPX files are provided in good faith, but neither the author nor the publisher accept responsibility for their accuracy.

EMERGENCIES

The pan-European emergency telephone number 112 is used to call for assistance throughout the Canary Islands, linking with the police, fire service or ambulance, for a response on land or at sea. The Guardia Civil telephone number is 062 and it is most likely that they would be involved in mountain rescue, as they generally patrol rural areas. All the islands have a hospital and all the towns have pharmacies. Walk safely, with due care and attention to avoid accidents and injuries. A good insurance policy will cover against medical fees and repatriation, but be sure that the provider will offer cover for a trek such as the GR131, which ventures into remote country and mountainous terrain.

LANZAROTE

A path leaves Máguez and crosses a gap to reach Haría (Stage 1)

LANARZOTE
73km (45¼ miles) 5 days

The GR131 begins with an easy coast-to-coast traverse through Lanzarote. Most of the route follows quiet roads, dirt roads and tracks, though there are occasionally some more rugged, narrow paths. Although Lanzarote features many fine volcanic cones, the route doesn't climb any of them, but stays low on their slopes. The route almost climbs to the highest point on the island, at Peñas del Chache, but the summit is occupied by a military installation and is therefore out of bounds to visitors.

The route through Lanzarote wanders easily from village to village and town to town, passing areas currently under cultivation, or areas that have been cultivated in the past. There is no natural running water on the island, so apart from sparse rainfall, or condensation from mist on higher ground, water has to be piped into these areas. What appears to be barren, black volcanic ash is actually surprisingly fertile, and in some areas it is dug from the mountains and spread thickly on poor ground.

As the trail through Lanzarote is so easy, and as so many places are cultivated, it isn't easy to pitch a tent unobtrusively. However, there are excellent bus services to and from many parts of the route, so it makes sense to operate from a base. By staying in Arrecife, preferably within walking distance of the bus station, it is possible to commute to and from the GR131 and complete the trail carrying only a day pack in as little as five days. Onward transfer from Lanzarote to Fuerteventura is easy, with fast and frequent ferries covering the short distance between the islands.

TRANSPORT

Intercity bus services allow all the start and finish points of each daily stage to be reached easily, and buses are sometimes available at points during each stage. Although Sunday services are less frequent, there are particularly good services to Teguise from around Lanzarote, serving a popular Sunday market. Check the website for full details of services, www.arrecifebus. com, or tel 928 811 522.

TOURIST INFORMATION

The main tourism website for Lanzarote is www.turismolanzarote. com. Tourist information offices are located at the airport, Arrecife, Teguise and in the tourist resorts.

Airport, tel 928 820 704
Arrecife, tel 928 802 884
Costa Teguise, tel 928 592 542
Teguise, tel 928 845 398
Puerto del Carmen, tel 928 510 542
Playa Blanca, tel 928 518 150

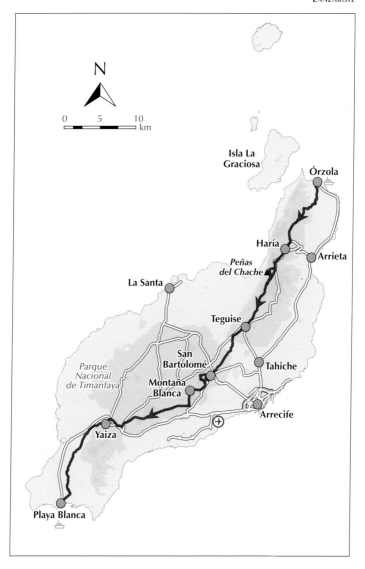

STAGE 1
Órzola to Haría

Start	Harbour, Órzola
Finish	Bus stop, Haría
Distance	12km (7½ miles)
Total ascent	470m (1540ft)
Total descent	190m (625ft)
Time	3hr 30min
Terrain	Mostly rugged slopes but crossed by good roads and tracks. Some short paths are steep and rugged.
Refreshments	Bar-restaurants at Órzola, Máguez and Haría.
Transport	Intercity bus 9 serves Órzola from Arrecife, Teguise and Punta Mujeres. Intercity bus 7 serves Máguez and Haría from Arrecife, Teguise and Punta Mujeres.
Accommodation	Limited choice in Órzola and Haría.

The GR131 leaves the remote village of Órzola by road, passing rugged terrain and an unusual area planted with aloe vera. A gradual ascent into the rugged Malpaís de La Corona, a protected Natural Monument around a volcanic cone, features small vineyards. Fertile black-ash fields are passed near the village of Máguez, before the route crosses a hill to reach the neighbouring village of Haría.

ÓRZOLA

The road-end village of Órzola is busy whenever ferries arrive and depart, serving the nearby island of La Graciosa. It is a pity that the GR131 doesn't include La Graciosa, but there is nothing to stop keen walkers adding a pre-amble around the island before their trek. Órzola offers a little accommodation, a few bar-restaurants, a couple of shops, an ATM, bus and taxi.

The GR131 starts at a map-board across the road from the ferry ticket office and bus stop. No matter who else is coming and going, it is unlikely that anyone else will be standing at the map-board, ready to walk for one month through the Canary Islands to distant El Hierro. Simply follow the road, Calle La Quemadita, straight through **Órzola**. You might spot small plaques on some of the buildings, reading 'Camino Natural de Órzola a Playa Blanca'. Get used to the style of these, as they will be seen on signposts and waymark posts all the way through Lanzarote.

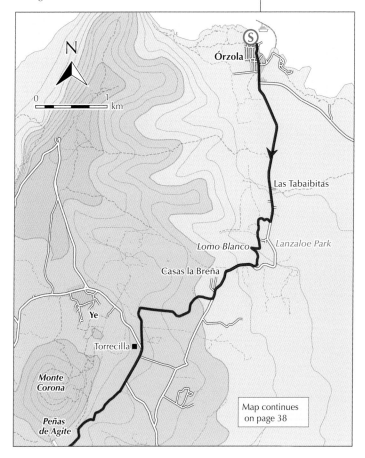

Map continues on page 38

Keep straight ahead at a road junction as signposted for Haría, and use the pavement provided. After passing a bus shelter and a chapel note the Km1 marker beside the road. With other markers appearing every kilometre, it is easy to keep track of progress. The broken lava flanking the road bears rubbery *verode* and *tabaibal*, as well as crinkly *aulaga* plants. The pavement continues through the little village of **Las Tabaibitas**, then runs out at the Km2 marker.

Pass another bus shelter then turn right as signposted along a track through rugged terrain. Turn left at a junction and the track is stone-paved for a while, giving way to a more rugged path, which quickly reaches a dirt road. ◄ The GR131 climbs a track that becomes more rugged as it makes a pronounced zigzag on **Lomo Blanco**. At a higher level it becomes a rugged path, then

Turning left gives access to the Lanzaloe Park and an interesting trail through areas planted with aloe vera, tel 928 524 335 www.lanzaloe.com.

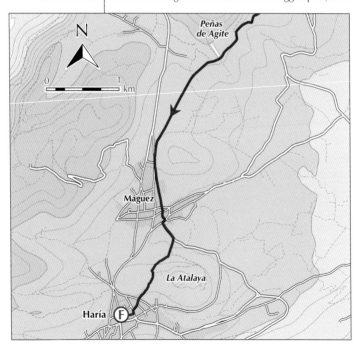

runs more easily parallel to a road. When the path runs out at a signpost near **Casas la Breña**, follow the road past the Km4 marker to another signpost.

Turn right and follow a dirt road uphill, passing a few odd houses, some very rugged areas dotted with *calcosa* bushes, and a few small vineyards. There are tracks to right and left, but stay on the main dirt road throughout, climbing as marked. The Km5 marker is passed on the ascent and, just after you reach a signposted junction with a tarmac road, the Km6 marker is passed. ▸ The prominent early 20th-century mansion of **Torrecilla**, above the road, and the jagged rim of Monte Corona catch the eye.

Follow the road downhill until it bends left, and keep straight ahead as signposted along a dirt road. This crosses the slopes of **Monte Corona**, where loose ash is bound by *calcosa* bushes. Avoid other tracks at junctions and always keep straight ahead as marked. A couple of pits have been excavated on the slope, then a shoulder is crossed at around 360m (1180ft), where a couple of stone-built water stores have been constructed near the Km8 marker. Simply follow the dirt road gently downhill,

The striking mansion of Torrecilla on the slopes of Monte Corona

Turning right along the road leads to the village of Ye and the Restaurante Volcán de La Corona.

39

passing fertile ash fields to reach a tarmac road at the top end of the village of Máguez. A range of shapely hills leads the eye ahead to the highest point on Lanzarote – Peñas del Chache.

While following the road down through **Máguez**, fork left at a junction as marked. Go straight through a crossroads at the bottom, and straight through a staggered crossroads to follow Calle las Cruces. Turn right at a junction as marked, then left to follow a road away from the village. ◄

There is a bar and an art gallery off-route.

Follow the road past flat fields until it is possible to turn right along a track. This soon gives way to a narrower path that becomes quite rough and stony as it climbs, passing the Km11 marker. There are signposts as the path joins a dirt road at 334m (1096ft), beside the hill of **La Atalaya**. Turn right and walk downhill, joining a tarmac road to continue past houses in **Haría**. Go through a crossroads and keep straight ahead along Calle Molino, turning left when signposted. You will see bus stops ahead, but turn right just beforehand, to reach the Km12 marker at the foot of a rather plain church tower, at around 280m (920ft).

HARÍA

At this point, trekkers will either catch a bus or head for their accommodation in the village. Either way, it is worth wandering around the centre. A tree-lined pedestrian street becomes quite busy on Saturdays when the Mercado Artesanal is in progress, with food and craft stalls offering local produce. The village has a bank with an ATM, bar-restaurants, shops, bus and taxis. It is also home to a museum dedicated to the artist César Manrique, which you will pass further along the GR131. The land around the village features an abundance of palm trees. It was once fashionable to plant two palm trees whenever a boy was born and one when a girl was born.

STAGE 2
Haría to Teguise

Start	Bus stop, Haría
Finish	Ayuntamiento, Teguise
Distance	13km (8 miles)
Total ascent	360m (1180ft)
Total descent	340m (1115ft)
Time	4hr 30min
Terrain	Mostly easy roads, dirt roads and tracks, as well as a couple of steep and rugged paths on the ascent and descent.
Refreshments	Bar-restaurants at Haría and Teguise, Restaurante Los Helechos off-route near Peñas del Chache.
Transport	Intercity bus 7 serves Haría from Arrecife, Teguise and Punta Mujeres. Intercity buses 7, 9 and 10 link Teguise with Arrecife, while buses 52 and 53 link Teguise with La Santa. Additional buses serve Teguise on Sunday from many parts of Lanzarote.
Accommodation	Available in Haría and Teguise.

This stage climbs almost to the highest point on Lanzarote, but the summit of Peñas del Chache is occupied by a military installation and is out of bounds to visitors. Despite this, there are wonderful and extensive views if the day is clear. A fairly direct descent leads to the lovely and ancient town of Teguise, whose narrow, cobbled streets are made for wandering and exploring.

Start at the bus stop beside the church in **Haría**, on La Plaza de Haría. The Km12 marker is at the foot of the rather plain church tower. Walk away from the church along a tree-lined street, turning left and then right at the end to reach the attractive Plaza de La Constitución. The Ayuntamiento is here, with map-boards and a signpost beside the adjacent library.

Most visitors turn left to follow Calle César Manrique, but the GR131 runs straight ahead, turning left later as signposted along Calle Ángel Guerra. The road crosses a

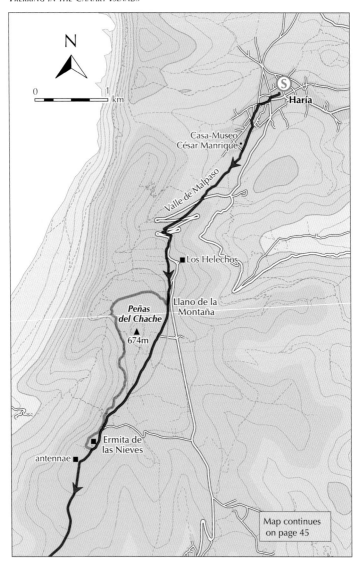

concrete dip, then a right turn leads along Calle César Manrique to the **Casa-Museo César Manrique**.

> The artist **César Manrique** left his mark around many parts of the Canary Islands and beyond. His house is a remarkable construction built into rugged lava and surrounded by exotic gardens. It opens daily at 1030, so any trekkers who visit will be unlikely to be walking again until noon. For details, contact tel 928 843 138 www.fcmanrique.org.

Keep straight ahead at a junction to follow a dirt road from the Km13 marker. Keep right at a signposted junction, following a track that climbs a cultivated slope. Cross a main road, but don't be tempted to follow it, as it is very convoluted and it is easily three times the length of the GR131. A partly stone-paved path climbs further, passing the Km14 marker and crossing the road again at a sign for **Valle de Malpaso**. Climb another stretch of the path, which zigzags steep and rugged, passing a road bend, then crossing the road yet again. The path is stone-paved as it climbs a short way to cross the road one last time. ▶ It is worn to bare rock as it climbs a wonderfully scrub-covered slope to reach a dirt road. Turn left to follow the road past a couple of houses. Turn right along a tarmac road and follow it to a signposted junction with another dirt road at **Llano de la Montaña**.

Turning left up the road leads to the Bar Restaurante Los Helechos and its fine viewpoint terrace.

Alternative route adds 1km (½ mile), 10m (30ft) ascent/descent, 30 min
In clear, dry, calm weather, follow the dirt road signposted for **Peñas del Chache**. This bends right as it climbs, passing a goat farm. It touches 630m (2065ft), then keep left as it descends gently. Pick up and follow a path along a cliff edge well below the summit of Peñas del Chache. You need to be careful, but the views are wonderful in clear weather. The path eventually follows a drystone wall to a cliff-edge car park, where a dirt road can be followed up to the whitewashed chapel of **Ermita de las Nieves**, sitting on a rounded hill surrounded by palm trees.

*Peñas del Chache
is the highest point
on Lanzarote*

Main route continues

The GR131 continues straight along the tarmac road, passing black-ash fields and little buildings, well below the prominent radome that sits on top of Peñas del Chache. At 674m (2211ft) this is the highest point on Lanzarote. The road, however, rises only to 620m (2035ft), just after passing the Km16 marker. The descent is gradual and easy, with views ahead of a whitewashed chapel on a rounded hill surrounded by palm trees. The route stays on roads, turning right at a junction to climb a short way to the **Ermita de las Nieves**. There is a large dirt car park alongside, and it is worth walking to an abrupt edge to sample views well into the middle of Lanzarote, and from coast to coast. The city of Arrecife and the little town of Teguise are also in view.

A broad dirt road descends from a map-board, signpost and the Km18 marker, soon passing a military installation bearing an array of **antennae**. Pass two signposts while following the dirt road down a barren slope and also pass the gentle hump of **Pico de Maramajo**. The kilometre markers count to Km21, then a rugged path is signposted down to the right. The path is often trodden to bare, bright rock, equipped with a few stone steps. It becomes an easy, level track as it passes a white building beside a black-ash field. Pass the Km22 marker and walk through a track intersection, keeping right of the substantial ruin of the **Ermita de San José**.

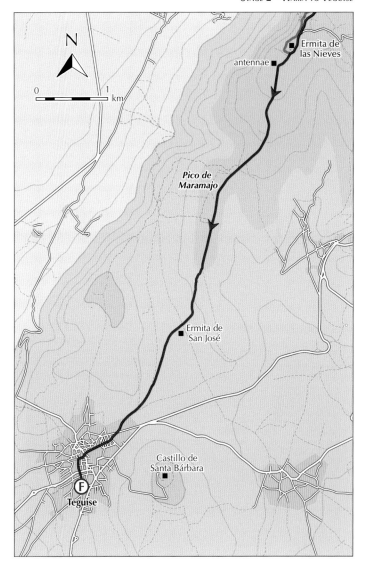

A dirt road runs level through a broad valley containing a mixture of fertile and barren areas. Simply keep straight ahead at junctions, joining a road to pass a football ground on the outskirts of **Teguise**. Turn right at a road junction, but keep left of a large, triangular garden in the middle of a complex junction of roads. Watch carefully to spot marker plaques at eye level on buildings, following Calle Puerto y Villa de Garachico down into the town. The Km24 marker is passed just after Las Nieves Supermercado. ◄ Walk further downhill and turn left at a signposted junction where the roads are block-paved. Turn right at the Aloe Museum, then later left along Calle Santo Domingo. This leads straight to the Ayuntamiento and bus stops, around 300m (985ft). However, feel free to take any route through town.

Note the large marketplace to the left, which becomes very busy on Sundays.

TEGUISE

The centre of this ancient town has a maze of cobbled streets. A busy Sunday market is served by buses from many parts of Lanzarote. There is a bank with an ATM, post office, accommodation, bar-restaurants, shops, crafts, buses and taxis. The hilltop Castillo de Santa Bárbara, dating from the late 16th century, operates as a pirate museum. For details contact tel 928 594 802 www.museodelapirateria.com.

A popular Sunday market takes place in Teguise

STAGE 3
Teguise to Montaña Blanca

Start	Ayuntamiento, Teguise
Finish	Montaña Blanca
Distance	15.5km (9¾ miles)
Total ascent	270m (885ft)
Total descent	300m (985ft)
Time	4hr 30min
Terrain	Gently sloping at first, with easy dirt roads and tracks, becoming a little steeper later, though still using easy paths and tracks.
Refreshments	Bar-restaurants in Teguise and San Bartolomé. Teleclub (bar) in Montaña Blanca.
Transport	Intercity buses 7, 9 and 10 link Teguise with Arrecife, while buses 52 and 53 link Teguise with La Santa. Additional buses serve Teguise on Sunday from many parts of Lanzarote. Intercity buses 16, 20, 52 and 53 link San Bartolomé with Arrecife. Bus 32 links San Bartolomé and Montaña Blanca with Arrecife and Playa Honda.
Accommodation	A good choice in Teguise and San Bartolomé, but nothing available in Montaña Blanca.

The walk downhill from Teguise is easy, crossing a broad agricultural saddle in the middle of the island. The gradual climb to the bustling village of San Bartolomé is also easy, and as this point might be reached before midday, it is worth continuing onwards. However, the route becomes remarkably convoluted and the neighbouring village of Montaña Blanca has little to offer visitors.

Leave the Ayuntamiento in **Teguise**, as if following Calle Guatatiboa to Arrecife. However, turn right down Calle Siemprevivas, passing the Km25 marker to leave town. Turn right along the dirt road called Calle Crisantemo. Just before reaching a tarmac road, turn left down a narrow, walled path to join the road. Turn left and walk down to the Km26 marker and a signpost, turning right to follow a

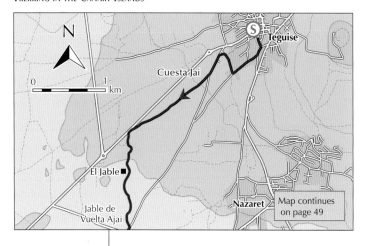

dirt road. Pass fields of black ash and a couple of houses, while drawing closer to a busy road on **Cuesta Jai**.

Just before reaching the road, turn left along a track, reaching a few tiny houses and cultivation plots. Follow a path as marked, reaching a signpost and the Km28 marker. Join a track beside a house called **El Jable** and continue across **Jable de Vuelta Ajai** to join a road. Turn right and pass through a nearby crossroads to follow a very broad dirt road. This rises onto old lava flows at **El Volcán**, though these have been extensively quarried, leaving unsightly areas to the right. To the left, lie expanses of grass dotted with crinkly *aulaga*, where several areas have been ploughed and planted. ◀ There are several track junctions, and while many bear marker posts, some don't, but progress is simply a matter of rising gradually south-westwards.

The dirt road passes between two rocky tors, and the curious hilltop house of **Casa Natura** is seen ahead. Old volcanoes jostle along the skyline, with white villages dotted around the landscape. After passing the Km32 marker a small noticeboard explains about cultivation alongside the Camino del Jable. Marker posts lead past fields and the dirt road gives way to the tarmac Calle Juan de Bethencourt.

Unlike the black-ash fields passed earlier, the soil here contains windblown sand from the distant coast.

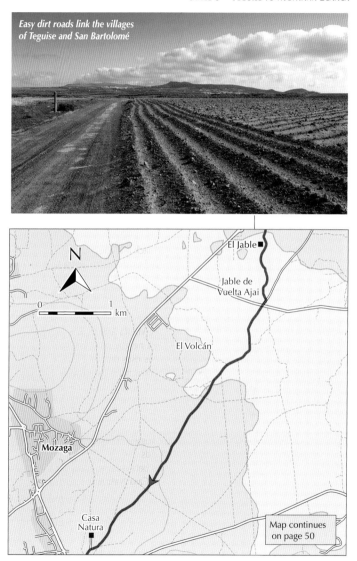

Easy dirt roads link the villages of Teguise and San Bartolomé

Map continues on page 50

Turn left along a busy road in **San Bartolomé** and use the first pedestrian crossing to reach the Pastelería Lolita. Turn left along the busy road, then right as signposted along a brick-paved stretch of Calle Rubicón.

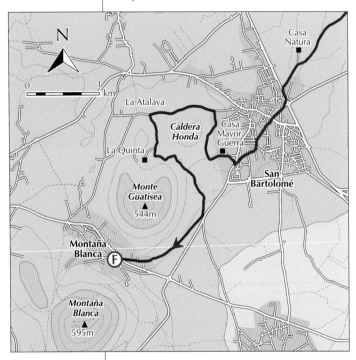

SAN BARTOLOMÉ

This busy village offers plenty of options for food and drink, and a number of bus services pass through it. There are banks with ATMs, post office and shops. Accommodation tends to be in the form of apartments. The Museo Tanit is interesting, tel 928 802 549 www.museotanit.com. Reaching the village from Teguise might only constitute a morning walk, so it is worth continuing if only to cover more distance. The route to Montaña Blanca is remarkably convoluted.

Turn right to continue along another busy road, which is still the Calle Rubicón. Marker plaques are sparse and aren't easy to spot, but follow the road straight through a mini-roundabout crossroads. Reach the attractive Plaza León y Castillo, where there is a signpost and map-board. Follow the road onwards, which is still Calle Rubicón, through another crossroads, keeping right at a roundabout near an old windmill. The road eventually passes another mini-roundabout, then there is a right turn at a road junction with a signpost and map-board. The road quickly gives way to a brief, stone-paved path through a garden beneath the 18th-century house of **Casa Mayor Guerra**. ▶

This was once the home of a military figure and it now operates as a museum, tel 928 522 351.

Keep left to pass below the house and the paved path gives way to a gritty path, climbing from a signpost and passing the Km35 marker. Stay on the clearest path, which climbs and bends right. Follow only the GR131 markers and signposts, avoiding local waymarks. The route makes a circuit around the volcanic cone of **Caldera Honda**, following a track to 335m (1100ft), then descends to a road junction on the outskirts of San Bartolomé. Turn left to follow the rather lumpy road uphill, passing a couple of houses at **La Atalaya**. ▶ The road descends and a signpost points left along a dirt road.

There are views of a black ash landscape largely occupied by vineyards.

The middle part of Lanzarote as seen from Caldera Honda

There is a gentle ascent past a few little houses, then keep left at a junction near **La Quinta** to pass over a gap beside **Monte Guatisea**. The dirt road descends past a few more houses, almost reaching a busy road near a large white building. Keep right to follow another dirt road, Calle San Bartolomé, gradually uphill. It reaches a map-board just before following a tarmac road into **Montaña Blanca**. Go straight through a crossroads to find Calle Lomo de Tesa. There is a bus stop at the top and another at the bottom, around 270m (885ft). Bus services run in opposite directions at different times, but all buses ultimately reach Arrecife, which is useful as there is nowhere to stay in the village and nowhere offering food and drink apart from the local Teleclub bar.

STAGE 4
Montaña Blanca to Yaiza

Start	Montaña Blanca
Finish	Church, Yaiza
Distance	17km (10½ miles)
Total ascent	390m (1280ft)
Total descent	480m (1575ft)
Time	5hr
Terrain	Mostly easy roads, dirt roads and tracks from village to village, with occasional paths. Gentle slopes give way to rugged lava towards the end.
Refreshments	Small bar at Conil. Bar-restaurants at Uga and Yaiza.
Transport	Intercity bus 32 serves Montaña Blanca from Arrecife and Playa Honda. Intercity bus 34 is an 'interior' service, linking villages such as Conil and La Asomada with Tías, where other buses can be caught. Intercity bus 60 links Uga and Yaiza with Playa Blanca and Arrecife. Bus 161 links Yaiza with Playa Blanca and the airport.
Accommodation	Sparse around Conil and La Asomada, but more options around Uga and Yaiza.

Although this stage passes a number of villages, facilities are sparse. The walking is easy and mostly follows roads, dirt roads, tracks and occasional paths. Mountains are stacked alongside the trail and there are options to climb some of them. Towards the end, a remarkably easy path crosses a savage lava flow and it is trodden on a daily basis by camels!

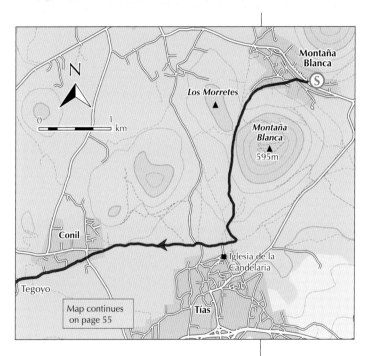

Start on Calle Lomo de Tesa in Montaña Blanca. If arriving by bus, it will stop either at the top or bottom or the road, depending on which way it is running. The Km40 marker is halfway down the road. Go straight through an unmarked crossroads at the bottom, then keep left to go up Calle el Especiero. When the road suddenly turns left, keep straight ahead up a dirt road. Pass a map-board near the last house in the village. A track and path continue

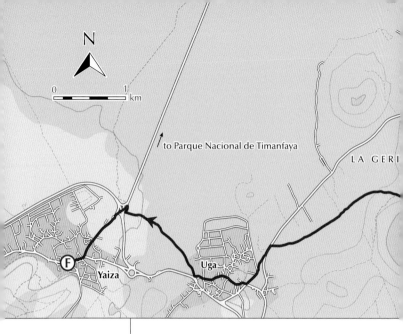

up through a valley, reaching another track. Turn left to follow the track through a gap between the mountain of **Montaña Blanca** and **Los Morretes**. The gap is at 399m (1309ft) and the view is interesting as it includes four islands – Graciosa, Lanzarote, Lobos and Fuerteventura.

Walk down the track, but don't go near any houses near the bottom. Instead, turn left at a track junction and walk down to a signpost beside a dirt road above the northernmost suburbs of **Tías**. Turn right and pass the Km43 marker and another signpost where a road rises from a church, the **Iglesia de la Candelaria**.

Keep straight ahead along the broad dirt road, which is the Camino La Villa. Follow a short stretch of a road called the Camino Fajardos, then turn left up another broad dirt road, the Camino Peña del Asiento. This climbs gently, with rounded old volcanic cones rising to the right, while farms and built-up areas lie down to the left. The dirt road gives way to tarmac then, when a map-board is reached, keep left at a road junction to pass

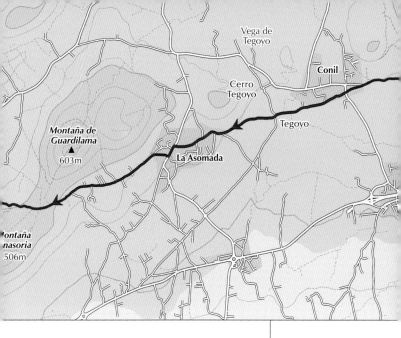

houses in **Conil**. When a crossroads is reached, the route runs straight ahead, passing the Km45 marker. ▸

The road called Camino Callao II descends past a few houses to pass through a staggered crossroads at a signpost and the Km46 marker at **Tegoyo**. Follow the road straight uphill, noticing a concrete slope on **Cerro Tegoyo**, where rainwater is channelled into cisterns. The road levels out at the Km47 marker, passing a map-board and houses on the way to a main road in the village of **La Asomada**.

Turn left downhill, then turn right as signposted up Camino La Caldereta. The houses gradually thin out and the tarmac gives way to a dirt road. Avoid all turnings and simply climb to reach a gap between the steep-sided **Montaña de Guardilama** and the gentler **Montaña Tinasoria**. ▸ The trail reaches 412m (1352ft) and the dirt road runs down past the Km50 marker. Black ash stretches far away towards the red volcanic peaks of the Parque Nacional de Timanfaya. Countless thousands of pits have been excavated, protected by semi-circular walls to enable

Turn right uphill at the crossroads, where a small bar might be open beside a church.

Signposts indicate paths to both summits, for those inclined to climb them.

55

Montaña de Guardilama and the black-ash vineyards of La Geria

vines to grow. This is the wine-producing region of **La Geria**, which looks barren, but is surprisingly fertile.

Follow the dirt road downhill, then it rises and falls gently. Simply avoid all tracks leading off it, eventually reaching a map-board and signposts beside a busy road. Turn left along the road, then turn right as signposted down a short dirt road. Turn left again along Calle Los Arenales, then right at a junction along Calle La Agachadilla, entering the village of **Uga**. If a bus is needed, the stop lies to the left beside a play park, otherwise follow Calle Joaquín Rodríguez through the village. There is a shop and a couple of bar-restaurants, as well as weekend markets. The road rises and almost joins a busy main road.

Turn right as signposted along the dirt road called the Camino de los Camellos. Pass through a modern vineyard then continue along a narrow path that easily crosses an incredibly rugged, jagged lava flow. The path is coated in camel dung, deposited by hundreds of camels as they make their way to and from the Parque Nacional de Timanfaya, morning and afternoon. ◄

If the camels are heading your way, step onto the lava and let them pass!

The path becomes a track leading to a house, whose access road leads down to a busy roundabout. Follow the main road under a bridge, go round another roundabout and continue straight into the village of **Yaiza**. A junction is reached beside an old school – the Antigua Escuela. If a bus is needed, turn left to find bus stops near a supermarket, otherwise turn right to walk to the church in the village centre, around 180m (590ft).

The camel path across rugged lava between Uga and Yaiza

YAIZA

Yaiza has bar-restaurants, shops, a bank, accommodation and a number of art and craft outlets. There are bus services and sometimes a taxi is parked beside the church.

STAGE 5
Yaiza to Playa Blanca

Start	Church, Yaiza
Finish	Harbour, Playa Blanca
Distance	15.5km (9¾ miles)
Total ascent	80m (260ft)
Total descent	260m (855ft)
Time	5hr
Terrain	An easy dirt road gives way to rough and stony tracks and paths across rugged, stony slopes. Easy road-walking at the end through a busy resort.
Refreshments	Bar-restaurants in Yaiza and Las Breñas. Plenty of choice in Playa Blanca.
Transport	Intercity bus 60 links Yaiza with Playa Blanca and Arrecife. Bus 161 links Yaiza with Playa Blanca and the airport. Fred Olsen, Naviera Armas and Líneas Romero operate ferry services between Playa Blanca and Corralejo.
Accommodation	Plenty of choice around Playa Blanca.

On the map, this looks like an easy stage, running direct to the finish with no major ascents or descents. It does indeed start very easily, but later there are some quite rough and stony tracks and paths. It can't be hurried without risking a twisted ankle, so if you are trying to make haste to catch a particular ferry, it might be better to let it go and use the next sailing.

Start at the church in the centre of **Yaiza** and simply follow the main road gently downhill in the direction of Playa Blanca. There seem to be no markers for the GR131, but eventually you pass the Km57 marker and a map-board. Also pass a bus shelter at **Aljibe de Yaiza** then turn left as signposted up a broad flight of 79 stone steps. Turn right to follow a crunchy, red-dirt road gently downhill while enjoying extensive views across jagged black lava to the red-tinted volcanoes of the Timanfaya

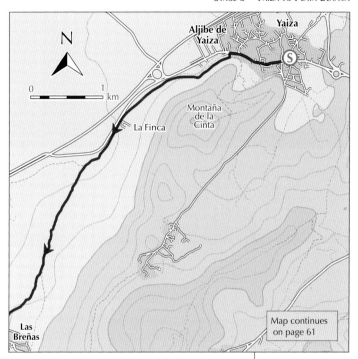

Map continues
on page 61

National Park. A busy main road is in view, equipped with a very large and attractive roundabout. The dirt road becomes grey gravel, passing the Km59 marker near an enclosed area of trees and buildings at **La Finca**. Montaña de la Cinta and the neighbouring peaks of Los Ajaches are otherwise steep and barren.

The dirt road descends gently into a broad and dusty valley. A number of vague tracks rise into the stony wastes beyond, but keep watching for markers to stay on course. The lumpy, stony ground is awkward underfoot and views become ever more extensive. The track becomes much clearer once it is flanked by tumbledown stone walls. A concrete-walled enclosure is reached at the Km62 marker, around 150m (490ft). A dirt road quickly

One of Lanzarote's decorative roundabouts outside Yaiza

reaches a signpost at a roundabout on a road. Turn right down the road, which is a quiet dual carriageway with palm trees separating the lanes. A complex junction is reached at a bus shelter and restaurant.

Follow the only road that runs almost level through the village of **Las Breñas**, passing below the Plaza San Luis. ◄ Turn right as signposted gently down Calle Víctor Fernández Gopar, drifting gently downhill, and keep straight ahead at another junction where there is a bus shelter. Later, turn right along Calle Los Roques, passing houses with fine cactus gardens. Turn left as signposted at a triangular junction down the very short Calle La Granja. This quickly gives way to a dirt road, and almost immediately a signpost points down a steep and rugged track on the right. Go past a walled goat enclosure at the Km64 marker and pass the little hill of **Los Roques**.

There is another restaurant above the plaza.

A rough and stony path descends gently across an extensive stone-strewn slope. It has become better trodden since being marked as the GR131, passing a notice drawing attention to the archaeological site of **Poblado del Terminillo**. Keep following the path downhill, uphill and downhill again, reaching a level area at the Km67 marker, where the white **Casas del Terminillo** lie to the left. A track joins a dirt road at the corner of a drystone wall. A nearby signpost points right along a rugged track crossing a level expanse of stony ground.

The track reaches a very broad dirt road and continues straight along another dirt road, passing the Km68 marker. The houses at **Hoya de la Yegua** are surrounded

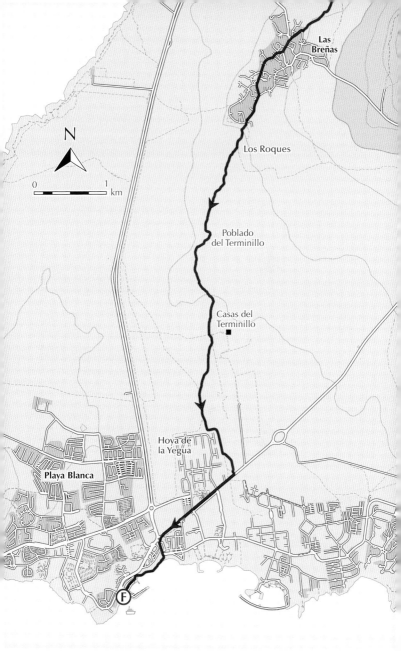

N

0   1
km

Las Breñas

Los Roques

Poblado
del Terminillo

Casas del
Terminillo

Hoya de
la Yegua

Playa Blanca

F

The end of the GR131 on Lanzarote at Playa Blanca

by a tall white wall that seems quite unbroken. The dirt road turns left to pass between the wall and unsightly heaps of building rubble. Turn right around a corner of the wall, then a path on the left is marked, leading to a very busy main road. ◀

This is odd, as the dirt road reaches the main road more directly.

Turn right to follow the main road, quickly picking up a pavement alongside. There are hardly any GR131 markers, but the road passes a roundabout to reach another roundabout in **Playa Blanca**, where a signpost points towards the town centre. ◀ Simply walk straight down to another roundabout, to find the final GR131 map-board just to the right. Go down the very short, pedestrianised Avenida Marítima to reach a sandy beach.

The bus station lies just beyond the roundabout.

Turn right along the attractive promenade, which has stout chain fences alongside, passing numerous bars and restaurants. Go down a flight of steps and follow a road round the harbour. It is unlikely that you would have to wait more than an hour or so for a ferry to link with the next stage of the trail on Fuerteventura.

LANZAROTE TO FUERTEVENTURA

Linking the last stage of the GR131 on Lanzarote with the first stage of the GR131 on Fuerteventura is a simple matter. Three ferry companies sail between Playa Blanca and Corralejo. Simply find out which one is sailing next, buy a ticket and get straight across in as little as 25 minutes, and no longer than 45 minutes. No other link between any two of the Canary Islands is likely to be accomplished so quickly and easily.

Fred Olsen, tel 902 100 107 www.fredolsen.es
Naviera Armas, tel 902 456 500 www.navieraarmas.com
Líneas Romero, tel 928 596 107 www.lineasromero.com

FUERTEVENTURA

Casas de Pecenescal   9 km
Casa de Risco del Paso   12 km

La Pared   6 km

Signposted tracks cross the desert-like expanse of El Jable (Stage 12)

FUERTEVENTURA
164km (102 miles) 9 days

The GR131 crosses the Islote de Lobos before making an eight-day coast-to-coast traverse through Fuerteventura, which is the longest of the Canary Islands. Most of the route uses quiet roads, dirt roads and easy tracks, but there are also more rugged paths through mountain gaps or along mountain crests. Although Fuerteventura was once a notable producer of cereal crops, these days abundant parched terraces and exhausted plots far outnumber cultivated areas and some areas resemble deserts.

The route through Fuerteventura makes its way from village to village and town to town, and some places are a long way apart. Some villages have useful facilities, but some have very little to offer passing trekkers, while the bustling resorts of Corralejo and Morro Jable have everything. In a few places, simple trail shelters offer rudimentary respite from strong sun and wind, and in some remote places it might be possible to pitch a tent without attracting attention.

Operating from bases at Corralejo, Puerto del Rosario and Morro Jable might be possible, commuting to and from the trail by bus, but some services to villages in the middle of the

Betancuria is one of the oldest settlements in the Canary Islands (Stage 10)

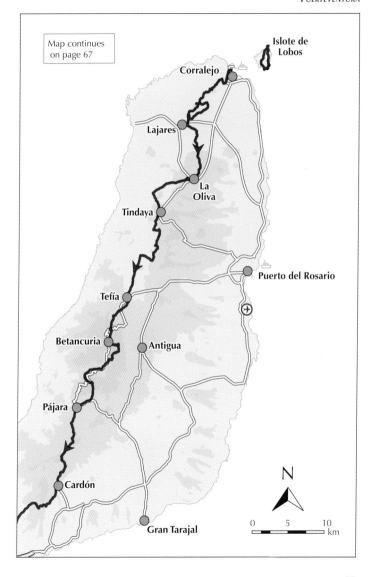

Map continues
on page 67

Islote de
Lobos

Corralejo

Lajares

**La
Oliva**

Tindaya

Puerto del Rosario

Tefía

Betancuria   **Antigua**

Pájara

N

Cardón

0   5   10
km

Gran Tarajal

65

A path climbs high above Valle de Santa Inés to Corral Guise

island don't have the best timetables. Accommodation in the form of small hotels and B&Bs is sparse, but there are options at the end of most of the suggested stages, otherwise it will be necessary to leave the route to seek lodgings and return the following morning. Plan ahead by two or three days if possible, and if lodgings can't be secured at any point, check the bus timetables to places offering more options.

Onward transfer from Fuerteventura to Gran Canaria involves navigating one of the largest gaps in the Canary Islands where careful attention is needed due to limited bus and ferry timetables. It could take a whole day to effect a transfer, so be sure to study options well in advance.

TRANSPORT

Tiadhe bus services allow the start and finish points of each daily stage to be reached, but bear in mind that some buses run frequently, from early morning until late at night, while other routes have fewer buses, operating at awkward times.

If planning to use buses to commute to and from the GR131, study the timetables carefully. Check the website for full details of services, www.tiadhe.com or tel 928 855 726.

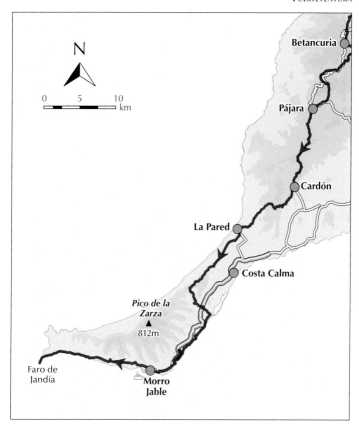

The main tourism website for Fuerteventura is www. visitfuerteventura.es. Tourist information offices are located at the airport and in the main towns and tourist resorts.

- Airport, tel 928 860 604
- Puerto del Rosario, tel 618 527 668
- Corralejo, tel 928 866 235
- Betancuria, tel 928 549 604
- Pájara, tel 928 540 776

STAGE 6
Islote de Lobos

Start/finish	El Muelle, Islote de Lobos
Distance	8km (5 miles)
Total ascent/descent	150m (490ft)
Time	2hr 30min
Terrain	Easy walking along good tracks and paths.
Refreshments	Small restaurant at El Puertito. Plenty of choice in Corralejo.
Transport	Ferries serve Lobos from Corralejo. They usually leave Corralejo at 1000 and the last departure from Lobos is usually 1600, but be sure to double check on the day of your visit, tel 638 572 971 or 616 986 982 www.navieranortour.com.
Accommodation	None on the island, but plenty of choice in Corralejo.

The ferry from Lanzarote and Playa Blanca berths at Corralejo. There are two options at this point. One is to walk into town and continue straight along the GR131 through Fuerteventura. However, there is a short stretch of the GR131 on the little island of Lobos, for which another ferry service must be used. Tickets can be bought from one of the booths around the harbour.

The route through Lobos is short and easy, but double the distance needs to be walked in order to return to the ferry. With this in mind, and to avoid retracing your footsteps, this stage offers a circular walk around the island, taking in the hamlet of El Puertito, views of Las Lagunitas marshes and the small Faro Martiño lighthouse, before returning along the GR131.

CORRALEJO

Corralejo used to be a simple fishing village, but it has expanded to become a thriving tourist resort. It is quite likely that at least one night will be spent in town and there is abundant accommodation. Corralejo could be used as a base while exploring the island of Lobos and the GR131 as far as La Oliva, but afterwards the bus connections would become awkward, unless Fuerteventura's capital, Puerto del Rosario, was used as a base for a few days.

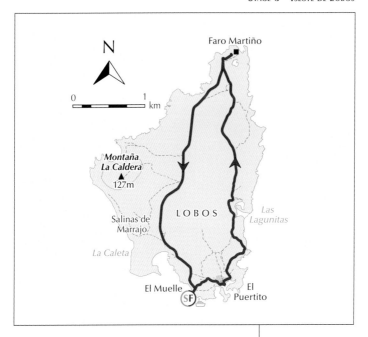

Ferries land at **El Muelle** on Lobos. Notices and signposts abound, and a visitor centre focuses on the wildlife of the island. There is a map-board for the GR131 and a signpost points left, but save that route for the return. Instead, turn right and follow a dirt road to a huddle of little houses at **El Puertito**. There is a small restaurant and another visitor centre.

After leaving the settlement, you reach another signposted junction. Turn right, then, after the path rises a short distance, go down boulder steps and past marshy pools. Just before reaching a hut, turn left up a path to reach a noticeboard overlooking the marshes of **Las Lagunitas**. Continue straight along the path as signposted, without turning off at any junctions. The route passes a few stone huts before reaching a junction where there is a GR131 map-board and signpost. A broad and clear path

The Faro Martiño at the northern end of the Islote de Lobos

Views stretch back to Lanzarote and through Lobos to Fuerteventura.

climbs onto a little hill crowned by a small lighthouse, the **Faro Martiño**. ◄

Walk back down to the map-board and signpost to start following the GR131. There is a rocky cove to the left, then the broad path runs almost through the centre of the island. Halfway along the path, you reach a junction where another path heads right to climb **Montaña La Caldera**. Feel free to climb it if you have an extra hour to spare. There are two more features of note to the right of the GR131. First is a path leading to the disused **Salinas de Marrajo**, closely followed by the popular sandy beach of La Caleta. The path quickly leads back to the visitor centre and **El Muelle**.

STAGE 7
Corralejo to La Oliva

Start	Plaza Patricio Calero, Corralejo
Finish	Church, La Oliva
Distance	25km (15½ miles)
Total ascent	480m (1575ft)
Total descent	260m (855ft)
Time	8hr
Terrain	Mostly easy roads, dirt roads and tracks, although some short stretches of path are rugged underfoot.
Refreshments	Plenty of choice in Corralejo, Lajares and La Oliva.
Transport	Tiadhe bus 8 links Corralejo, Lajares and La Oliva.
Accommodation	Plenty of choice in Corralejo and also options in Lajares and La Oliva.

The bustling resort of Corralejo quickly gives way to winding dirt roads and rugged *malpaís* slopes around a range of volcanic hills. There is an option to peer into the crater of Calderón Hondo, or stay on the GR131 to reach the village of Lajares. Another rugged *malpaís* area is crossed on the slopes of Montaña de la Arena before a gentle descent to La Oliva.

Start on the Plaza Patricio Calero in **Corralejo**, where there is a map-board and signpost. The signpost points towards Calle de Milagrosa, where a right turn leads up a pedestrianised stretch of Calle Lepanto. The rest of this narrow street leads to the broad and busy dual carriageway of Avenida Juan Carlos I, close to the bus station. Cross the road to a medical centre, or Urgencias, turning left to follow the road all the way out of town. There is a roundabout on the edge of town, then the road rises to the **Estrella del Norte** roundabout, which bears a sculpture of a sailing boat.

Turn right up a road then take the second turning on the right. Walk through a failed urbanization project, following roads with lampposts, pedestrian

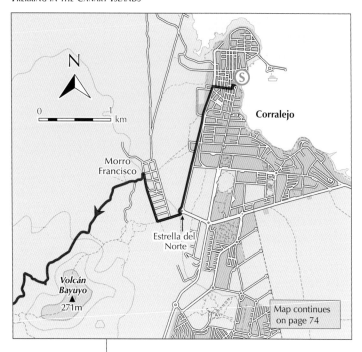

Map continues
on page 74

crossings and speed limits, but no houses. Turn left as signposted up a winding dirt road, passing a white-walled reservoir. ◀ The road rises to a noticeboard on **Morro Francisco**, which offers a few notes about the geology and wildlife of the area. The road rises further then drops a little, where a sign points left for 'Caldera'. A short, easy climb allows a view into a crater on the slopes of **Volcán Bayuyo**.

Follow the winding, undulating road onwards, passing a notice pointing out features in view, such as hills and a little cave. There are a few small buildings dotted around, including one that sells goat's cheese, at the Ganadería y Quesería Las Calderas. Still further up the road, a stone-paved path to the right offers an alternative to the GR131.

The road is dusty and is used by vehicles, including jeep safaris.

Alternative route to Lajares saves 2km (1¼ miles) with additional 50m (165ft) ascent/descent

The stone-paved path is the SL FV 2, marked with green and white posts. It passes a notice that explains about the area around **Calderón Hondo**. Turn right at a junction, then left at another junction. ▸ The path is steep and rocky, but quickly reaches a viewpoint looking into the crater of Calderón Hondo, from 230m (755ft). There is a telescope for studying the view. Descend and keep right at path junctions until you join a track at a turning area and follow it to cross the reddish slopes of **Montaña Colorada**. The track has a stone-paved path built into it and descends to a road where it re-joins the GR131.

The GR131 follows the broad dirt road round the slopes of **Caldera de Rebanada**, descends past a whitewashed ruin, then bends right near some ash quarries. Watch for a signpost pointing right along a track, around 115m (380ft). The track is called Calle Juanita and it rises a little to pass a trail **shelter** – one of several built along the route. The surface becomes stony and a little house lies to the right. A notice later names a number of nearby volcanic peaks visible from **Cuesta de la Caldera**.

Easy walking on dirt roads passes old volcanoes above Corralejo

Right leads to a curious stone-built hut.

73

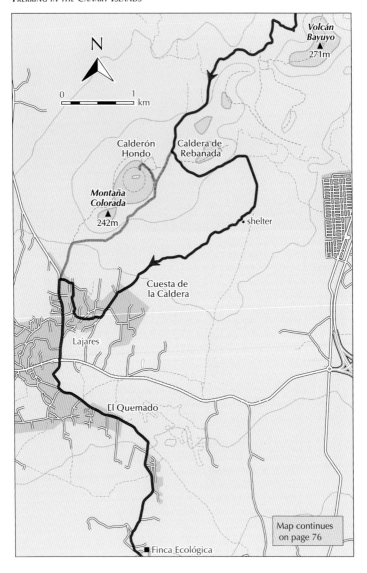

The track joins dirt road leading away from a house, then descends between two modern houses. A tarmac road is joined and followed past more houses. Turn right at a signposted junction, then right again at a waymarked junction, along Calle Fragosito. This becomes a dirt road, which turns left at a junction to lead to a tarmac road, joining the alternative route at a map-board and signposts. ▶ Turn left to follow the road past a bar-restaurant and continue down past a football ground to pass a roundabout on a busy road. Keep straight ahead as signposted for the GR131, or turn right into **Lajares** for food, drink and buses.

Camel rides are offered here on weekdays.

The road onwards is Calle Los Quemados, running beside a gently sloping plain. Turn left as signposted at a junction and the plain lies to the left at **El Quemado**, while houses gradually thin out on the right. There are junctions, but always keep straight ahead until signposted right up Calle Gavias Nuevas. Tarmac gives way to a dirt road after passing a few houses with palm and cactus gardens. The dirt road rises fairly direct, but a bendy stretch can be avoided by using a short waymarked track.

A dirt road leads away from Lajares to the Malpaís de la Arena

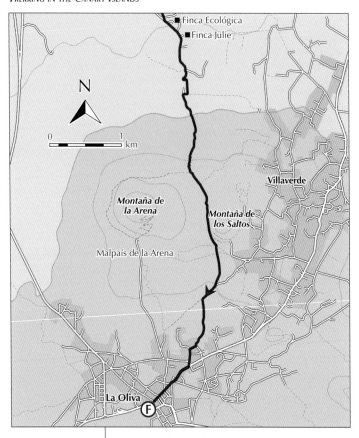

Pass the **Finca Ecológica** and **Finca Julie**, then continue uphill, keeping left of a tiny house. Turn right along its access track, then quickly left as signposted up another track. The slopes are protected as the Malpaís de la Arena, formed of materials from the eruption around 10,000 years ago of **Montaña de la Arena**. The path joins a track at a trail shelter, then the track crosses a broad gap at almost 290m (950ft). ◄ Descend a little, join a dirt road and continue straight ahead, passing **Montaña de los Saltos**.

Look back to see the Islote de Lobos and Lanzarote.

76

There is a view of the nearby village of **Villaverde** and a couple of windmills, but the GR131 is signposted to the right. An old track flanked by stone walls was once exceptionally stony, but a fine ash path has been constructed down it. Follow it across one dirt road and keep right while clipping a bend on another dirt road. The path later joins a dirt road, which becomes tarmac. Turn right at a signposted junction and left at a waymarked junction, heading straight for a busy road. Cross over and turn right to follow a palm-fringed pavement into **La Oliva**. The bus stops are just before you reach the church, around 220m (720ft).

LA OLIVA

Fuerteventura was under military rule from 1708 to 1849. The 18th-century Casa de los Coroneles at La Oliva served as a residence for the military governors and is now a museum, tel 928 868 280 www.lacasadeloscoroneles. org. The village has a market and arts centre, as well as accommodation, bar-restaurants, pizzeria and good bus services to Lajares and Corralejo.

STAGE 8
La Oliva to Tefía

Start	Church, La Oliva
Finish	La Cancela, Tefía
Distance	17.5km (11 miles)
Total ascent	210m (690ft)
Total descent	230m (755ft)
Time	5hr 30min
Terrain	Mostly easy dirt roads at gentle gradients.
Refreshments	Bar-restaurants at La Oliva and Tindaya. Bar-restaurant at Tefía.
Transport	Tiadhe bus 8 serves La Oliva from Corralejo. Tiadhe bus 7 serves Tindaya from Lajares, La Oliva and Puerto del Rosario. Tiadhe bus 2 serves Tefía from Puerto del Rosario and Betancuria.
Accommodation	Options in La Oliva, but very little in Tindaya and Tefía.

Almost the whole of this stage is spent following broad dirt roads across extensive, stony semi-desert. The splendid little 'sacred' mountain of Montaña Tindaya catches the eye most of the day, and it can be climbed from the GR131. Bear in mind that accommodation is sparse and buses off-route are infrequent, so it is worth spending time making sound plans for this and subsequent days.

Start at the church in **La Oliva**, where there is a map-board and signpost across the road. Follow a quiet road away from the main road, signposted for Cotillo and Lajares, passing the museum of Casa la Cilla. ◄ Watch for waymarks on lampposts and turn left along another road. Pass to the right of a curious building, the funeral home of Tanatorio Padrón, then cross a main road as signposted. A filling station with a shop and café stands to the left, while scantily clad statues stand in a palm grove to the right. Turn right along a road marked for La Villa de los Artistas. The road later bends left, reaching open spaces in the suburbs of La Oliva.

Go through a crossroads then, when the road bends left again, there are two dirt roads on the right. Take the

The museum is based in an old granary, tel 928 868 729.

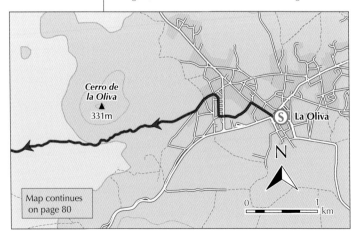

Cerro de la Oliva
▲
331m

S La Oliva

N

Map continues on page 80

0   1
          km

one furthest right, which has a marker post. The road undulates gently across the lower slopes of **Cerro de la Oliva**, with the pyramidal peak of Montaña Tindaya seen ahead, rising beyond a stone-strewn semi-desert. Descend gently along **Lomo de Herrera** and cross a broad valley. Rise gently past a goat enclosure and go straight through a dirt crossroads as signposted. Montaña Tindaya rises steep and rocky on the left, while another stone-strewn semi-desert stretches far away to the right. Pass a junction marked for Finca Esquinzo then turn left as signposted at the next junction. Pass other junctions as marked, until you reach a point where a path climbs **Montaña Tindaya**.

Often referred to as a 'sacred' mountain, **Tindaya** was held in high regard by the original Mahorero inhabitants of Fuerteventura. They carved curious *podomorfos*, or foot-shaped markings, into rocks around the summit of the 400m (1312ft) mountain. The late sculptor Eduardo Chillida identified this as the perfect mountain to have huge cubic caverns carved into it, looking out to the sea and sky. Naturally, people have diverse opinions about whether or not the project should go ahead.

The conical Montaña Tindaya is prominent for at least half a day

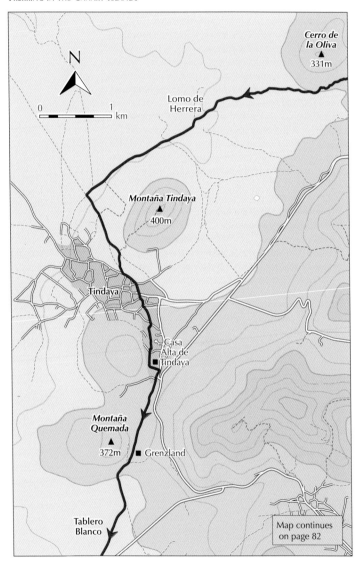

Map continues
on page 82

If not climbing the mountain, simply turn right at the next junction of dirt roads. Join an access road in a dip and follow it up to another road. The Bar-Restaurante Los Podomorfos lies to the right, otherwise turn left as signposted and follow the road straight into the village of **Tindaya**. The Bar González and a shop stand at a crossroads, and occasional bus services pass.

Follow the Calle de la Casa Alta straight up from the bar. Go straight through three crossroads while avoiding most of the houses in the village. Pass the Quesos Tindaya, and the road later bends left downhill. **Casa Alta de Tindaya** is on the left. ▶

Turn right at a road junction and keep right, effectively straight ahead, to go down a dirt road. This passes through a gap in the hills, and the rounded hill to the right is **Montaña Quemada**.

Notice a statue of the Spanish poet, novelist and playwright **Don Miguel de Unamuno**. He was exiled to Fuerteventura in 1924 for criticising the new government of General de Rivera.

The building has been restored and exhibits seek to explain Eduardo Chillida's vision for Montaña Tindaya, tel 928 865 616.

Paths and tracks stay low on the way to the village of Tefía

The dirt road passes **Grenzland**, the artist Edi Mann's home, which is described as 'an oasis in the desert'. Follow the dirt road downhill as marked, then over the white stony expense of **Tablero Blanco**. Drop to a road and cross over to follow another dirt road past a windpump.

Before reaching a house, turn left along a path that has been constructed on a gentle slope of stony scrub. It passes a house and joins a tarmac road. Turn right to follow it a short way past another house. It then continues as a dirt road which you follow up to a junction and a fence corner at the foot of a mountain range at **Rincón del Cercado**. ◄ Downhill, extensive stony plains are dotted with occasional houses or goat farms.

There are paths that allow these mountains to be explored.

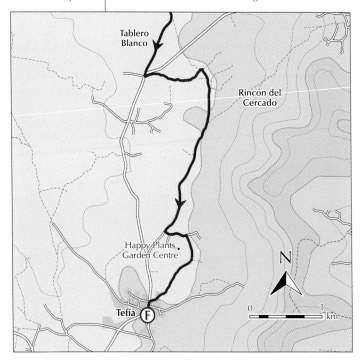

Follow the undulating dirt road onwards, until eventually a signpost points left up another dirt road. This passes the **Happy Plants Garden Centre**, climbing further and passing marker posts at junctions. The dirt road crosses a dip then rises to a tarmac road. Turn left to enter the village of **Tefía**, reaching a bar-restaurant and shop at La Cancela, with a bus shelter opposite, around 200m (655ft). Accommodation and bus services are sparse, so have a good plan in place before arriving here.

STAGE 9
Tefía to Betancuria

Start	La Cancela, Tefía
Finish	Bus stop, Betancuria
Distance	17.5km (11 miles)
Total ascent	530m (1740ft)
Total descent	340m (1115ft)
Time	6hr
Terrain	Mostly easy roads, dirt roads and tracks across stony plains and passing through villages. A more rugged path climbs steeply to a mountain gap, followed by a descent.
Refreshments	Café at the Ecomuseo La Alcogida. Bar-restaurants at Llanos de la Concepción, Valle de Santa Inés and Betancuria.
Transport	Tiadhe bus 2 links Tefía, Llanos de la Concepción, Valle de Santa Inés and Betancuria with Puerto del Rosario.
Accommodation	Very little all the way from Tefía to Betancuria.

There is an option to explore old farm buildings at the Ecomuseo La Alcogida on the way out of Tefía. After crossing stony semi-desert terrain, the route climbs gently from village to village, from Llanos de la Concepción to Valle de Santa Inés. The route crosses a mountain gap before dropping to the charming village of Betancuria. This is one of the oldest and most central settlements in the Canary Islands.

Leave the bus shelter opposite La Cancela by walking into **Tefía**, but almost immediately turn left off the main road, along a quiet road. Go straight ahead at junctions to reach a Canarian wrestling ring, or Terrero de Lucha, and the **Ermita de San Agustín**.

> **Canarian wrestling** is played out on a dirt floor. To win, a player only needs to keep their feet on the ground. If any other body part touches the ground, they lose. Wrestling involves three main moves – grabbing, blocking and deflecting – in order to beat an opponent.

There is an admission charge to explore the buildings, tel 928 175 434.

The road leads to a triangular junction planted with cactus. Keep right, and the tarmac gives way to a dirt road among some restored farm buildings. These are part of the extensive **Ecomuseo La Alcogida**. Cross the main road to find the reception building and a café. ◄

A sudden change of direction after passing the Molino de Tefía

> The **Ecomuseo La Alcogida** is a reconstructed farming village, where visitors can walk in and out of buildings, seeing what the houses and implements looked like a century ago. Sometimes, people may be in period costume, demonstrating bygone working practices.

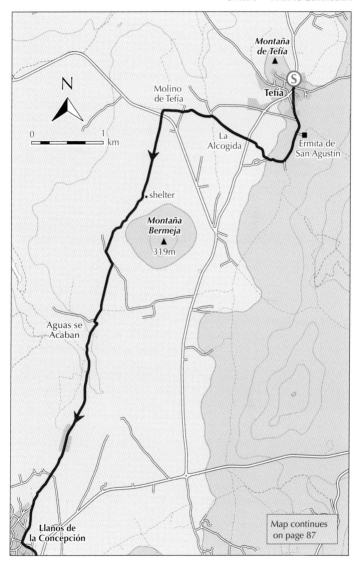

Map continues on page 87

85

If not stopping to explore the site, simply follow a dirt road onwards. Turn left up a tarmac road, which soon gives way to another dirt road leading to a fine windmill, the **Molino de Tefía**. There is also a small observatory nearby. The GR131 continues straight along a stony track over a barren plain, turning left at a signpost along a path leading to a road. Cross the road and continue along another track, still on a stony semi-desert plain. A trail **shelter** is reached at the foot of **Montaña Bermeja**.

The track runs past the mountain and passes close to a farm. Turn left along its dirt access road, then turn right along a track, passing a line of telegraph poles. Join another dirt road and turn right to follow it past acacia trees, keeping left at a junction to cross a gentle valley at **Aguas se Acaban**. The dirt road becomes a tarmac road, rising through an estate of widely spaced modern houses. Keep straight ahead at all road junctions, until a left turn leads to a little church, or *ermita*, in **Llanos de la Concepción**.

Shortly after passing the church, turn left down a track, then keep right to follow a path through tunnels beneath a new and an old road. ◀ The path joins a dirt road, and a right turn leads straight up through a dirt crossroads. Simply climb up the broad **Lomo de Tetir**, passing a fine windmill. Later, the dirt road runs parallel to the main road then joins it at a junction in the village of **Valle de Santa Inés**, where there are bar-restaurants, a shop and bus shelters.

If the Bar García, shop or bus stops are needed, head straight for the main road.

Cross over the main road, walk a short way along Calle Rey Abán, then turn left down Calle Coronel. The road crosses a valley, rises to a crossroads and passes straight through. The road leads to a number of farms in a green valley at **Vega Vieja**. Follow the road as marked and it gives way to a dirt road. This drops a little then rises and bends left. Leave it to continue straight up a track. This is worn to bedrock and later turns left, then a path quickly leaves it on the right. The path is rugged, but is unmistakable as it climbs steeply towards a gap in the mountains at **Corral Guise** around 600m (1970ft).

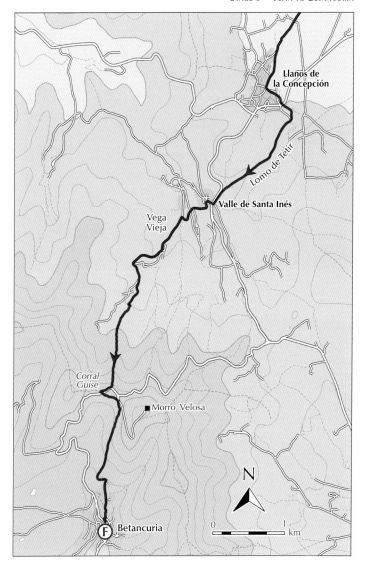

A fine windmill is passed on the gentle slopes of Lomo de Tetir

Walkers are in a minority on the gap, as a road also crosses it and motorists stop to enjoy the views in both directions. Two enormous statues represent two of the last **Mahorero chiefs**, Ayosa and Guise. Look back along the GR131 to the north, then cross the road and look south to see the village of Betancuria surrounded by mountains.

If the barrier on the road is closed, so is the restaurant!

Follow the path as signposted until it almost reaches another road. This serves a mountain-top restaurant at the **Mirador de Morro Velosa**, designed by César Manrique at 675m (2215ft). ◀

Simply follow the path downhill across a steep slope, and it gradually broadens to become a path, joining a road close to a substantial ruined convent. Walk down the road, later turning right and quickly left at junctions to reach GR131 signposts, a map-board and bus shelter in **Betancuria**, around 390m (1280ft). Spend any remaining time wandering around the streets of this charming and ancient village.

BETANCURIA

This is a very popular village during the day, but it gets very quiet in the evenings. Tucked safely into the hills, far from coastal invaders, it was founded in 1404 by Jean de Béthencourt and was once the capital of the entire Canary Islands archipelago, as well as Fuerteventura. It was destroyed by pirates in 1593 and ceased to be the island capital in 1834. Facilities include accommodation, bar-restaurants, shops, little museums and a rather limited daily bus service.

STAGE 10
Betancuria to Pájara

Start	Bus Stop, Betancuria
Finish	Church, Pájara
Distance	17km (10½ miles)
Total ascent	520m (1705ft)
Total descent	710m (2330ft)
Time	5hr 30min
Terrain	A mountain climb followed by an easy valley walk. Then, after a rugged climb to a mountain gap, there is another easy valley walk.
Refreshments	Bar-restaurants at Vega de Río Palmas. Plenty of choice at Pájara.
Transport	Tiadhe bus 2 links Betancuria and Vega de Río Palmas with Puerto del Rosario. Tiadhe bus 18 links Pájara and Gran Tarajal. Tiadhe buses 4 and 9 run infrequently, linking Pájara with Morro Jable by different routes.
Accommodation	Available in Betancuria, Vega de Río Palmas and Pájara.

On this stage the GR131 finally gets a taste of the mountains. Leaving Betancuria, the route climbs to the summit of Morro del Cortijo, which is the highest point on the trail through Fuerteventura. After descending to the village of Vega de Río Palmas, a rugged path crosses the mountain gap of Degollada los Granadillos. This stage ends with an easy walk linking the villages of Toto and Pájara.

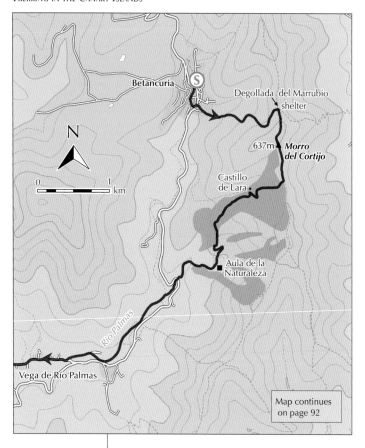

Starting from the bus shelter in **Betancuria**, walk up a stone-paved road to pass below the church. Keep walking straight ahead to find a flight of stone steps dropping to a narrow, paved path. When the path reaches a streambed, cross over and walk up a short tarmac road. Turn left and quickly right along stone-paved roads then cross the main road near an aloe vera shop. A stone-paved path leads to the well of Noria del Pozo de los Peña.

Follow a gravel path up to a road and turn left, then pass a signpost at the end of the road and continue up a track. Agaves stand beside the track throughout the ascent, with increasingly good views of Betancuria nestling among the hills. A trail **shelter** sits on the gap of **Degollada del Marrubio**, at 583m (1913ft). Turn right to follow a path straight uphill, reaching stone-built windbreak shelters on **Morro del Cortijo**, the highest point on the trail through Fuerteventura, at 637m (2090ft). ▶

From here there are views of the surrounding mountains and villages.

Follow a fence down to a gap at 569m (1867ft) and turn right to go through a gate. A track descends through a stunted, thirsty-looking plantation of pines. Turn left along a path that passes above buildings at the recreational area of **Castillo de Lara**. Go down and up a few log steps, then follow a path across a slope of pines and bushy scrub. Pass a pylon on a shoulder, followed by a ruin, then a low building. A track descends steeply, but instead of following it, turn left along a path for a more pleasant descent, overlooking the environmental education centre of **Aula de la Naturaleza**.

Turn right along a dirt road that follows a valley down to the main road. Just before reaching the road, turn right as signposted down a few stone steps, then follow a streambed through one of two tunnels beneath the road. It is stony underfoot and adjacent bushes are overgrown, but things improve quickly when you reach the broad bed of the Río Palmas, around 300m (985ft). The riverbed is used as a dirt road, serving a number of farms and houses. Watch on the left to spot a path signposted for Tiscamanita, but don't go that way. Later, watch on the left again to spot notices and signposts, indicating road access into the village of **Vega de Río Palmas**, should you wish to make a detour to visit the church or restaurant.

The dirt road continues further along the riverbed, but when the main road crosses, join it and turn right to follow it through the rest of the straggly village. A sign points right for a traditional bakery, and the road later passes the **Casa de la Naturaleza**, which offers food, drink and accommodation. Go down to a dirt car park where there are signposts indicating your options.

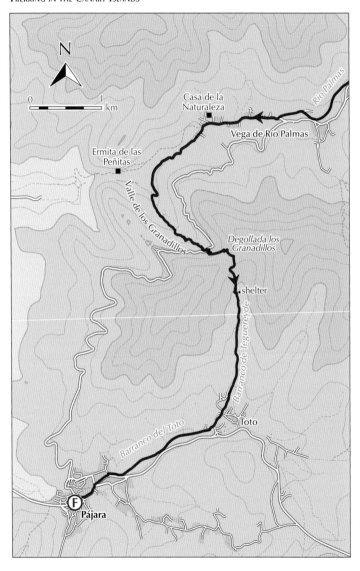

A popular path leads from the car park, through the valley to reach the top of an awesome rocky gorge. The tiny, whitewashed **Ermita de las Peñitas** has long been a place of pilgrimage for the inhabitants of Fuerteventura. However, to avoid the risk of accidents in such a remote place, a church was built in Vega de Río Palmas for the benefit of less sure-footed pilgrims.

The road passes the last few houses in the village, as well as a turning area for buses. It finally ends among a few cultivated patches, giving way to a track. Follow the track, but turn right up a rugged path. This climbs through the **Valle de los Granadillos**, crosses a scenic road, then zigzags further uphill to reach a small drystone shelter on the gap of **Degollada los Granadillos**, at 479m (1572ft). Go straight down the path on the other side, which is often worn to bedrock and flanked by impressive *tabaibal*. You reach a trail **shelter**, where the path becomes much easier underfoot.

An easy road-walk beyond Vega de Río Palmas

93

The GR131 stays low in a barranco between Toto and Pájara

Simply follow the path gently down through the **Barranco de Teguereyde**, crossing a couple of footbridges over small gullies. Follow a wall beside cultivated areas, joining a track, dirt road and tarmac road while approaching the top end of **Toto**. The road crosses a rise then runs straight downhill, passing through a crossroads near a church in the middle of the village. Calle Cuesta de San Antonio runs further downhill, but turn right as signposted down another road, and step onto a dirt road that runs along the dry riverbed of the **Barranco de Toto**, around 250m (820ft).

Stay low on the broad dirt road, passing farms and fields while approaching a built-up area. The riverbed runs parallel to a main road, then a signpost points left, indicating a few steps up to the road. Turn right to follow the road to a roundabout, then continue into the tree-shaded centre of **Pájara**. A map-board and signpost are located near the church, around 200m (655ft).

PÁJARA

The town is old, and while it suffered extensive damage during an invasion in 1593, it didn't suffer the total destruction meted out to Betancuria. The carvings above the entrance to the church of Nuestra Señora de la Regla are an intriguing mix. Pájara offers accommodation, a bank with ATM, bar-restaurants, shops and bus services.

STAGE 11
Pájara to La Pared

Start	Church, Pájara
Finish	Hotel, La Pared
Distance	26km (16 miles)
Total ascent	750m (2460ft)
Total descent	910m (2985ft)
Time	9hr
Terrain	Easy roads and dirt roads at the start and finish, with some good mountain paths in the middle. However, some paths are steep, rugged and vague in places.
Refreshments	Bar at Cardón. Bar-restaurants at La Pared.
Transport	Tiadhe bus 18 links Pájara and Gran Tarajal. Tiadhe bus 4 is an infrequent service linking Pájara with La Pared and Morro Jable. The Hotel La Pared operates a shuttle bus to and from Costa Calma.
Accommodation	Limited options in Pájara and La Pared.

This is a long and difficult stage, but you could break it at the halfway village of Cardón if you organise a pick-up or taxi. It starts with a walk along a high mountain crest, followed by a traverse across mountain slopes. Speed can be increased towards the end as the route follows a broad dirt road. A gradual descent leads to La Pared, which is a resort village built between the mountains and the sandy desert of El Jable.

A map-board and signpost stand at a junction near the church in **Pájara**. Follow the road signposted for La Pared and Morro Jable, but keep left at the Bar Tasca to follow Calle la Cañada, passing through a crossroads where there is a GR131 signpost. Fork left along Calle los Geranios, which suddenly narrows, passing a traditional mill. Turn left at a junction to reach a cemetery, then continue straight along a dirt road.

Pass a trail **shelter** and follow the dirt road onwards through the **Barranco de la Cañada**. Turn left at a junction beside an enclosure and follow a track uphill. There are

a couple of signposts, but the aim is simply to follow the track uphill while keeping to a broad stony crest on **Morrete de Tío Gómez**. A small notice at 357m (1171ft) points out how agriculture is managed on such dry and stony mountains. A marker post later indicates a path heading right, which after a bit passes a ruined enclosure on a shoulder, then drop to cross the valley of **Barranco Hondo**. The rugged path climbs and eventually joins another vague track on the mountain crest. Simply turn right and stay on the gentle crest.

There are hardly any markers, but none are needed. You pass stone windbreak shelters and descend to the gap of **Degollada Honda**, at 401m (1316ft). Climb and continue along the undulating crest of **Filo de Tejeda**, crossing its 449m (1473ft) summit. The ground becomes more rugged and is strewn with dark, chunky rocks. Looking ahead, aim for a trig point on the summit of **Pasos**, at 481m (1578ft).

Watch carefully to follow the red and white paint marks and go down a few crude stone steps to go along a path across the northern flank of the mountain. There are green patches and flowers in rocky crevices, not seen elsewhere in these barren mountains. Reach the gap of **Degollada del Risco** at 454m (1490ft) and look

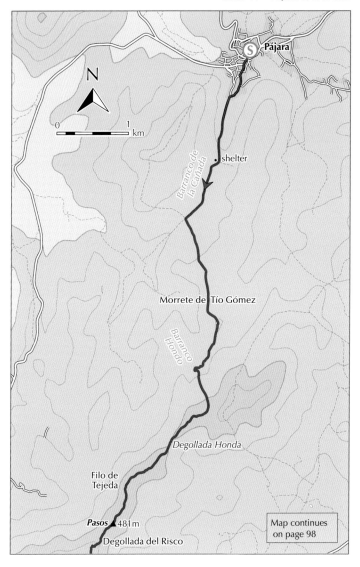

Map continues on page 98

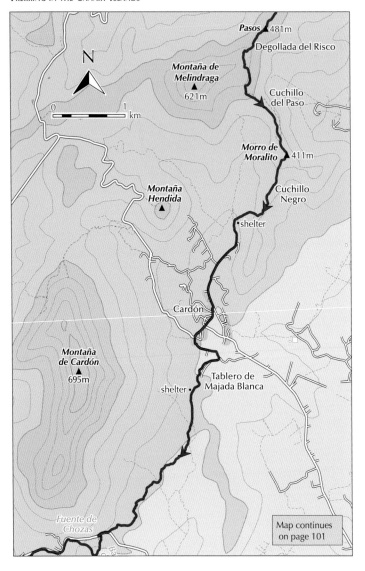

N

0   1
|___|___| km

Pasos ▲ 481m
Degollada del Risco

*Montaña de
Melindraga*
▲
621m

Cuchillo
del Paso

*Morro de
Moralito* ▲ 411m

Cuchillo
Negro

*Montaña
Hendida*
▲

•shelter

Cardón

*Montaña
de Cardón*
▲
695m

shelter •

Tablero de
Majada Blanca

*Fuente de
Chozas*

Map continues
on page 101

carefully for the line of a zigzag path up a steep slope of crumbling earth and stones. The mountain ahead is Montaña de Melindraga, but it isn't climbed. Instead, when a white-painted rock outcrop is reached, turn left to follow a path across a rugged slope. Reach a tumbled wall and follow it downhill, then continue following a fence. When the fence suddenly drops to the left, follow the path straight ahead.

Cross a track, descend, then follow the track along the crest of **Cuchillo del Paso**. There are scant markers as well as vague paths and tracks intersecting each other. Cross a gap and go over a rise, then cross another gap. The rugged hill ahead is **Morro de Moralito**. Keep left while climbing it, and the path passes between boulders while following a fence. There is a signpost and a couple of benches on top, around 400m (1310ft). ▶

The path descends, then follows a tumbled drystone wall beside the crest of **Cuchillo Negro**. Later, cross the crest as marked and follow a path downhill just to the left of a track. Veer left away from the track to reach a trail **shelter** at the foot of the slope. The path joins a dirt road and stays low in the Barranco de Bácher. Later, note a signpost on the right for El Tanquito, but don't go that

A clear path follows a fine crest towards the summit of Pasos

Enjoy views from the barren mountains to the cultivated plains, where there are several villages.

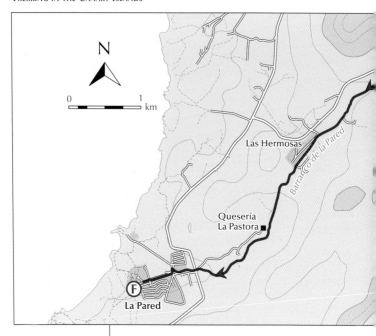

way. Further along the dirt road, turn right as signposted to follow a road into the little village of **Cardón**, around 200m (655ft). A bar stands beside a tiny church.

Go straight past a roundabout and bus shelter to follow a road uphill. Go through a crossroads to follow the bendy Camino de Julián Castillo Francés down past houses. Keep right as signposted at a junction and follow a dirt road uphill, reaching the shoulder of **Tablero de Majada Blanca**, around 230m (755ft), where you pass a trail **shelter**. A clear and obvious path has been constructed across the lower slopes of **Montaña de Cardón**, descending at first, crossing a succession of streambeds, then rising to run parallel to a mountain road at **Fuente de Chozas**, around 250m (820ft).

The road could be followed for 4km (2½ miles) in order to avoid some fiddly route-finding, but to stay true

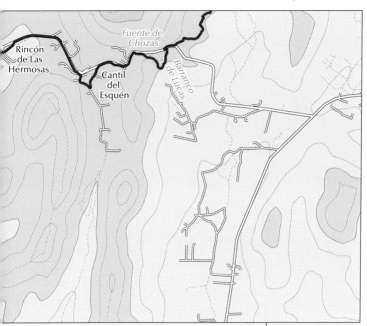

to the course of the GR131, cross the road as marked and pick up a track and path, dropping into the **Barranco de Lucas**. Join another track and climb, then as the track becomes rough and stony, switch to a parallel path as marked. When the mountain road is approached, walk parallel to it to pass the Finca de los Amigos. Continue alongside the road until a signpost points left down a dirt road, followed by a track, at **Cantil del Esquén**.

When you reach a road, turn right to follow it uphill and once again pick up paths running parallel to the mountain road, passing occasional houses and crossing their access roads while descending gently. Watch out on the left to spot an isolated, whitewashed stone-built gateway. Shortly after this, turn left along a dirt road and follow it gently downhill, soon crossing another road. The dirt road is plain and obvious as it runs through the broad

A fine path leaves a trail shelter high above the village of Cardón

Barranco de las Hermosas, then it rises gently to pass left of a little hill to reach the Estadio Benito Alonso at **Las Hermosas**, around 130m (425ft).

Keep following the dirt road gently down through the Barranco de la Pared and there is a choice of parallel roads. Follow either of them, later passing a goat farm where cheese can be purchased at the **Quesería La Pastora**. ◄ The dirt road continues onwards, then, just before joining a tarmac road, step to the right to spot three low tunnels beneath the road. Go through the middle one and, while the riverbed might be overgrown, follow it to another road.

The land is bare and waterless, so fodder and water have to be transported in for the goats.

Turn left along the road, then turn right at a roundabout on the outskirts of **La Pared**. A broad strip, rather like a linear park, lies between two parallel roads from one roundabout to another. Follow this strip, then continue straight ahead and notice the Hotel La Pared, on the right, around 40m (130ft).

LA PARED

This is a dry and dusty resort on the edge of a sandy desert. The hotel offers accommodation, food and drink, as well as having a grocery store and its own shuttle bus link with the resort of Costa Calma. There are a couple more bar-restaurants and a very limited bus service. Centuries ago, this area marked the division between the two Mahorero territories of Maxorata and Jandía.

STAGE 12

La Pared to Barranco de Pecenescal

Start	Hotel, La Pared
Finish	Barranco de Pecenescal
Distance	16km (10 miles)
Total ascent	290m (950ft)
Total descent	280m (920ft)
Time	5hr
Terrain	Gentle tracks and paths rise and fall on slopes of stones and sand.
Refreshments	None after leaving La Pared.
Transport	Tiadhe buses 1, 5 and 10 operate between Costa Calma and Morro Jable. They always stopped at the Barranco de Pecenescal when given a clear hand signal, but with the construction of a new road it is unclear whether they will continue to do so. If in doubt, be ready to call for a taxi in order to leave the route.
Accommodation	Limited at La Pared, then nothing, even at the end.

This whole stage is like a sandy desert criss-crossed with tracks and paths. Signposts and markers keep you on course throughout, and while some parts feature low, bushy scrub, in other parts be aware that windblown sand has buried some of the marker posts, making navigation trickier. At the time of writing a new road was being constructed at the end of this stage and a question mark hangs over whether buses will stop for passengers.

Start near the hotel in **La Pared** and follow the road straight to the edge of the resort, where there is a signpost and a dirt road. Set off along the dirt road, but almost immediately turn left and follow another dirt road uphill. There are marker posts at junctions, as well as a line of telegraph poles accompanying one sandy stretch uphill. Pass a noticeboard and reach a signposted junction. Soon afterwards, go through a dirt crossroads where there is a noticeboard about the Parque Natural de Jandía, around 110m (360ft).

Follow the dirt road straight ahead, almost level, and a signpost later points round a right-hand bend on **Piedras Negras**. Gradients continue to be gentle, but stone paving in places proves rugged underfoot. Follow the road in a ruler-straight line across a very broad dip on the scrub-covered crest, barely higher than 60m (200ft). Eventually, rise a little to pass through a signposted dirt crossroads. ◀ The way uphill is sandy, but occasionally stretches of the old stone-paved road are visible. Numerous marker posts appear alongside the road, leading round a bend while continuing the ascent, passing through a rather vague sort of crossroads on a sandy gap. ◀

The sandy road crosses the shoulder of **Alto de Agua Oveja**, around 190m (625ft). The marker posts continue to show the way uphill, eventually to 250m (820ft), but bear in mind that the sands of **El Jable** tend to drift, obscuring the posts on some occasions and revealing them at other times. When the sand has been scoured from the hillside, more stretches of the old stone-paved road can be seen on **Loma de la Ruda**. Descend to a stony crest around 200m (655ft) at **Degollada de Mojones**.

Turning left leads to the resort of Costa Calma.

This is close to the whirling turbines of the Parque Eólico wind farm.

104

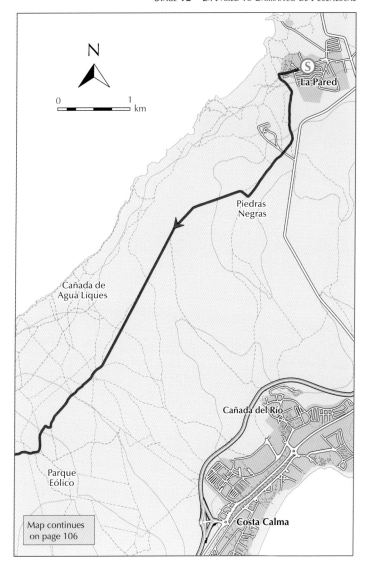

Map continues
on page 106

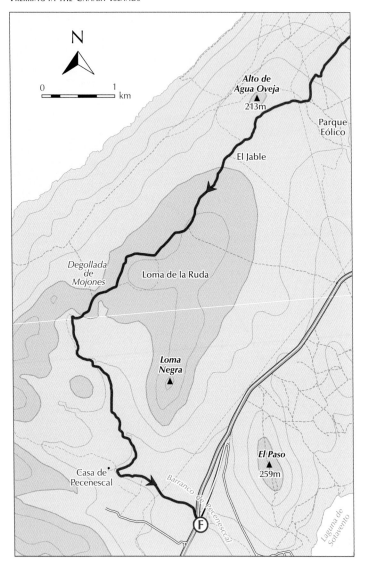

A signpost stands beside an old stone-paved stretch, and the dirt road descends into a stony riverbed. Follow this gently downhill but later step up from the riverbed and follow the dirt road roughly parallel. The road makes a sweeping bend as it passes a junction near the **Casas de Pecenescal**. Follow the dirt road away from the houses, later passing beneath three pylon lines. Continue the gentle descent towards a busy main road near the **Barranco de Pecenescal**, around 50m (165ft).

At the time of writing, a new main road was being constructed parallel to the existing main road, so pay attention to how the GR131 is marked and signposted. In the past, it was possible to catch buses by giving clear hand signals on deceleration lanes beside the old main road, but it is unclear if buses will continue to use the old road, or if there will be bus stops beside the new road. If you call a taxi, tell the driver to head for the Casas de Pecenescal, then be ready to stop the car as it leaves the main road. There are no facilities of any kind at the end of this stage, although it should be possible to pitch a tent discreetly. Naturally, all food and water need to be carried for an overnight camp.

Wind-blown sand threatens to bury marker posts high on El Jable

STAGE 13

Barranco de Pecenescal to Morro Jable

Start	Barranco de Pecenescal
Finish	Morro Jable
Distance	16.5km (10¼ miles)
Total ascent	400m (1315ft)
Total descent	450m (1475ft)
Time	5hr
Terrain	Stony ground covered in sand gives way to rocky slopes and beaches of sand and pebbles. There are several short, steep accents and descents, but most of the walking is easy, particularly towards the end.
Refreshments	Beach bar at Tierra Dorada. Plenty of choice around Esquinzo and Butihondo. Plenty of choice in and around Morro Jable.
Transport	Tiadhe buses 1, 5 and 10 operate between Costa Calma and Morro Jable. They always stopped at the Barranco de Pecenescal when requested, but with the construction of a new road it is unclear whether they will continue to do so. If in doubt, be ready to call for a taxi in order to join the route.
Accommodation	None at Barranco de Pecenescal but plenty of options from Esquinzo to Morro Jable.

This stage sees desert-like terrain give way to a rugged cliff coast, followed by a series of resorts culminating in the urban sprawl of Morro Jable. You will pass beaches, where beach goers have constructed and continually maintain numerous stone windbreak shelters to prevent themselves being sand-blasted on windy days. The route through Morro Jable passes an interesting saltmarsh, which is a haven for wildlife despite the number of holidaymakers.

This stage starts with a little uncertainty, as a new main road was being constructed at the time of writing. Hopefully, the GR131 will be clearly marked, whichever way it passes the main road in order to reach the nearby **Barranco de Pecenescal**. Originally, the route ran parallel

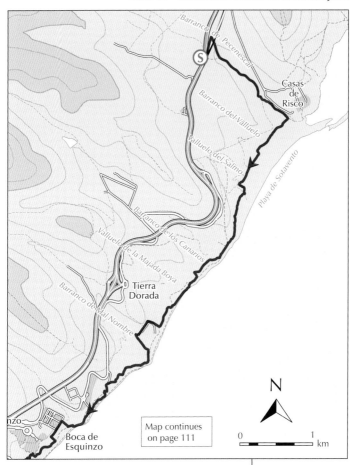

to the old main road, then passed beneath it using a tunnel. The broad and sandy bed of the barranco descends gently in a series of bends, eventually reaching a map-board and signpost beside an extensive sandy beach. Cars park here, and the nearest building is a surfing club, while the only other buildings nearby constitute the **Casas de Risco**.

Looking inland from the beach onto which the Barranco de Pecenescal emerges

There are several ascents like this during the day, none of them climbing 50m (165ft) above sea level.

Follow a path uphill as signposted, overlooking a saltmarsh and sandy beaches. ◄ Descend to cross the sandy **Barranco del Valluelo**. The path crosses another rise, then drops to the dry riverbed of Valluelo del Salmo. Walk towards a dirt car park to find the continuation of the path up another slope. The skeletal structure of an unfinished building complex looks completely out of place, and the GR131 goes down one of its broad, brick-paved access paths. Pass a road-end car park and cross the mouth of the **Barranco de los Canarios**. Climb and descend again, reaching the mouth of the **Valluelo de la Majada Boya**. Walk along a sand and pebble beach to reach a beach bar at **Tierra Dorada**.

Climb a flight of concrete steps and then left to follow a road past an abandoned, bulldozed area. Turn right to follow the road up to a junction then turn left, noticing another substantial unfinished development. A path leaves the road and descends to the mouth of the **Barranco de Mal Nombre**. Climb again, then drop into a small rocky valley, then keep right of a derelict building before dropping to a beach. After a short beach walk there are two options. Either keep walking along the beach, or climb a flight of steps towards a resort complex. If taking the latter, turn left after you have climbed 60 steps and contour across a steep sandy slope. Both options soon join again on the beach at **Boca de Esquinzo**.

Pass seawards of a house, which can be awkward when the tide is high. Just a short way along the beach, climb a concrete path, pass the Restaurante Marina Playa and go through a white-painted arch to reach a road in **Esquinzo**. Turn left up the road, Calle Volcán del Vayuyo, and walk straight ahead along a dirt road. Turn left downhill at a junction, picking up a fine, broad path along the brow of a rugged slope overlooking a beach at **Playa de Butihondo**.

Watch carefully to spot markers and a signpost as the route negotiates intersections of paths and tracks while crossing a valley. Another fine, broad path continues along the brow of a rugged slope, passing a resort development. ▶ On reaching the mouth of the **Barranco de Butihondo**, consider the state of the tide. If the water is low, continue along the rocky and sandy shore. If it is high, then follow a road up through the

Should you wish to visit the beach, which has a beach bar, paths offer access.

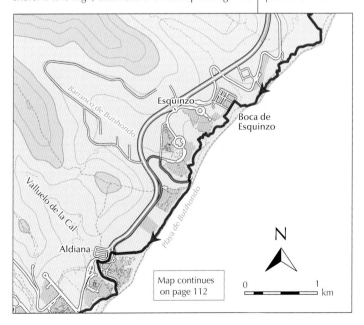

Map continues on page 112

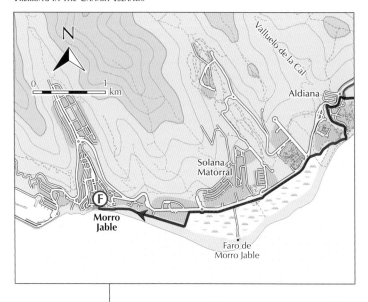

barranco, turn left to follow a road running parallel to a busy main road, eventually reaching **Aldiana** and a roundabout bearing sculptures of children. If the beach walk is taken, the GR131 is directed up a road to reach the same roundabout.

Leave the roundabout as if following the main road towards Morro Jable, but walk along a parallel dirt road, which drops into the **Valluelo de la Cal** and returns to the coast. Turn right to follow a footpath and cycleway, divided into lanes, with a dirt running track alongside. ◀ When an underpass is reached, don't go through it, but notice a signpost for Pico de la Zarza, which is the highest point on Fuerteventura. The footpath and cycleway run parallel to a busy main road, passing clearly marked beach access paths. The rest of the extensive saltmarsh between the built-up areas and the beach is protected and strictly off-limits. Note the skeleton of a sperm whale at **Solana Matorral**, where there is access to the lighthouse of **Faro de Morro Jable**.

Alternatively, follow the sandy beach onwards.

The route passes a protected marshland on the way through Morro Jable

Follow the footpath and cycleway towards **Morro Jable**, suddenly turning left to reach the sandy beach. Turn right to follow a promenade path shaded by palm trees. A brick-paved path rises and falls, passing above a sandy slope. The promenade levels out and narrows, passing lots of bars and restaurants. A reasonable point to finish would be where the promenade spans the mouth of a riverbed.

MORRO JABLE

This busy resort offers a full range of services, including plenty of accommodation. However, after days spent walking through barren countryside passing only occasional towns and villages, you might find there is too much hustle and bustle. If staying here, or using it as a base while walking the GR131, it is a good idea to find out where things are located among the winding road system. The bus station, for example, is high above the town, although there is a bus stop closer to the centre. The ferry-port is outside town and, if leaving in a hurry for the ferry, it is wise to have an exit plan, and maybe get hold of the phone number of a reliable taxi.

STAGE 14
Morro Jable to Faro de Jandía

Start	Morro Jable
Finish	Faro, Punta de Jandía
Distance	20.5km (12¾ miles)
Total ascent	280m (920ft)
Total descent	280m (920ft)
Time	6hr
Terrain	Fairly gentle, stone-strewn and sandy slopes, with only occasional short, steep ascents and descents.
Refreshments	Plenty of choice at Morro Jable. Bar-restaurants at El Puertito.
Transport	Tiadhe bus 111 serves Punto de Jandía twice a day. The final departure from the lighthouse is 1600, but it is wise to double-check. Morro Jable also has daily ferry services to Las Palmas in Gran Canaria.
Accommodation	Plenty available at Morro Jable, but nothing else afterwards.

The final stage of the GR131 through Fuerteventura continues the theme of stony semi-desert. A broad and popular dirt road runs from Morro Jable to the distant Punta de Jandía. Surprisingly, it has a bus service. The GR131 makes every effort to avoid the road, picking is way across stony slopes then following the coast. The lighthouse of Faro de Jandía is often in view, and the aim is to reach it in time to catch a bus. Be sure to have a good plan at hand for how you are going to transfer to Gran Canaria to continue along the next stage of the route.

Start on the lowest part of the promenade at **Morro Jable**, where a bridge spans the mouth of a barranco. Look uphill to spot a white-painted modern church tower. Walk towards it, turning right away from the promenade, then left and left again along the narrow passage of Peatonal La Chalana. A flight of 50 steps climbs a slope, then, by keeping left of the church tower, another 38

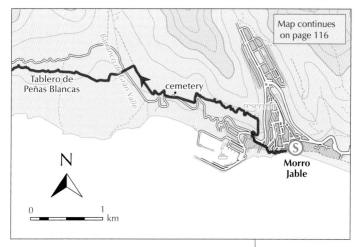

Map continues on page 116

steps climb to a road. Follow Calle Altavista, then turn left along Avenida del Faro, keeping straight ahead through a crossroads along Calle Los Atolladeros. At the end of the road a red concrete path leads to a main road. Cross over to reach a road marked for Cofete, then turn right to find a signposted path on a stony slope.

Follow the path straight uphill towards a concrete-walled **reservoir**. Turn left just before reaching it to follow a level, easy path across a steep slope of stone and broken rock, around 90m (295ft). The path lies on top of a water pipeline, and it runs level, despite the ruggedness of the slope. Painted pillars occur along its length. Watch carefully for a junction, where the path drops and almost reaches a road bend. However, it crosses a dry riverbed instead, climbs a little, then descends to the road just below a remote hillside **cemetery**.

Follow the road just past the cemetery, then pick up another clear path, crossing a couple of streambeds, then crossing a stony slope. Again, watch for a path junction, turn left and descend to cross a broad dirt road. There are a couple of farm buildings, a few withered trees and a grassy area. Keep right of them all and follow the path

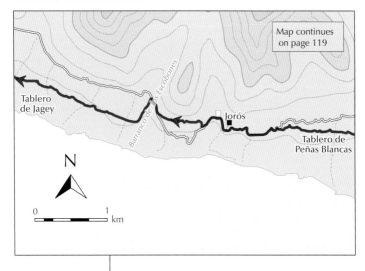

Map continues on page 119

Tablero de Jagey

Barranco de los Escobones

Jorós

Tablero de Peñas Blancas

N

0   1
               km

across the bed of the **Barranco de Gran Valle**. The path is obvious, but still bears marker posts where it crosses a few tracks on the slopes of **Tablero de Peñas Blancas**. Join and follow the main dirt road and pass scattered farm buildings and vegetated areas at **Jorós**.

Immediately after passing a final derelict house, turn right up a path, climb to a drystone enclosure and turn left to cross a slope. Pass slabs of sandstone around 70m (230ft) before descending to re-join the dirt road. Walk a short distance along it, then turn left as marked, down a path to the bed of the **Barranco de los Escobones**. Straggly 'tobacco' trees grow among the gravel. The path crosses the **Tablero de Jagey**, as well as crossing a number of tracks. Along the way, watch carefully to spot several peculiar cactus-like plants. ◄

Cardón de Jandía grows only in a few places on the Jandía peninsula, and nowhere else in the world.

After crossing the **Valle de los Mosquitos**, the path runs close to the rugged coastline from the **Baja de Juan Gómez**. Sometimes, the route follows paths, and at other times it follows tracks, crossing other tracks and dirt roads that serve the coast. Markers are sparse, but there is no need for them. Simply stay close to the coast, rising and

falling as you encounter low cliffs and dry valleys, seldom rising above 20m (65ft). A couple of large notices are passed around **Playa de las Pilas**, followed by a couple of small buildings near **Cueva de la Negra**.

A track leads past a huddle of vans and huts at **Casas de Salinas** and, despite there being several tracks along the coast and few markers, there should be no problem continuing through low, stony, sandy terrain, with an eye on a prominent wind turbine ahead. Pass **Punta de la Carnicería** and **Punta Percebe**, and when the wind turbine is close to hand keep right of it to join a tarmac road.

Turn left and follow the road past the desert-like expanse of **El Marrajito** and the tightly huddled village and caravans of **El Puertito**. There are a couple of bar-restaurants available. The road continues onwards, and if there is much traffic, you can walk alongside it. The lighthouse of Faro de Jandía stands on the **Punta de Jandía**, where a map-board and signpost mark the end of the trail through Fuerteventura. The twice-daily bus back to Morro Jable departs from the nearby bus stop.

Clear paths cross stony slopes on the Jandía peninsula

117

The route passes low cliffs and sandy and pebbly beaches

Looking west, it might be possible to spot **Gran Canaria**, but this is the largest gap between any two of the islands, measuring over 80km (50 miles) in a straight line. Sometimes, a puffy band of cloud gives away the island's location.

FUERTEVENTURA TO GRAN CANARIA

Linking the last stage of the GR131 on Fuerteventura with the first stage of the trek through Gran Canaria requires careful planning. First, it is necessary to catch the bus from Punta de Jandía back to Morro Jable. There are two buses per day, and depending on which one is used, the outcome for continuing the trek is different, as follows:

Walkers who start this stage very early in the morning could catch the 1200 Tiadhe bus 111 back to Morro Jable, which would enable a departure on the afternoon Fred Olsen (2hr) or Naviera Armas (2hr 50min) ferry to Las Palmas in Gran Canaria. On arrival in the big city of Las Palmas, walk from the ferry-port to the Santa Catalina bus station and catch Global bus 30, which takes about an hour to reach Maspalomas. After a night's accommodation, continue the trek the following morning.

Walkers who catch the 1600 Tiadhe bus 111 back to Morro Jable will have to spend a night in the resort, then sail early the following morning on the Fred Olsen (2hr) ferry to Las Palmas in Gran Canaria. Walk from the ferry-port to the Santa Catalina bus station and catch Global bus 30, which takes about an hour to reach Maspalomas. It should be possible to continue the trek and be able to finish the first stage during the rest of the day.

Fred Olsen, tel 902 100 107 www.fredolsen.es

Naviera Armas, tel 902 456 500 www.navieraarmas.com

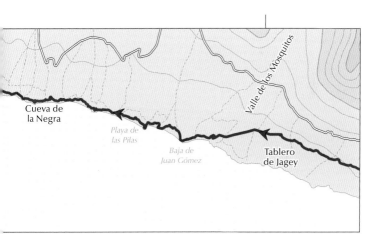

Looking back from the Faro de Jandía to El Puertito

GRAN CANARIA

View of the rugged north-western coast of Gran Canaria (Stage 19)

GRAN CANARIA
74km (46 miles) 5 days

Gran Canaria has not yet developed its stretch of the GR131, although for many years it has been assumed that it would run south to north through the island, making the most of the 'Cumbre', or high mountains of the interior. With this in mind, a route is presented in this guidebook which stays high and follows existing waymarked trails. Over the years, trails have been signposted on the island, backed up by a familiar 'European' marking system, only for them to be replaced by a system of waymarking peculiar to Gran Canaria. Both old and new markers will be observed while trekking through the island, including the S-54, PR GC 40, S-50 and S-90

Taking Maspalomas as a starting point, a broad and obvious barranco heads inland, with a waymarked trail alongside it. While this trail could be followed to Tunte, it is best to switch to a road-walk in order to gain height and enjoy extensive views. The end of the first stage is the little village of Ayagaures, and from there a fine trail can be followed over the mountains to Tunte. Continuing straight through the centre of Gran Canaria, you pass extensive pine forests and follow splendid mountain paths. Views take in incredible monoliths of rock and on

Clouds swirl around Roque Nublo, seen on the way to Cruz de Tejeda (Stage 17)

clear days it is possible to look ahead to the pyramidal peak of El Teide on the neighbouring island of Tenerife.

In order to stay high for as long as possible, the route passes through the delightful mountain village of Artenara and enters a remote and extensive pine forest at Tamadaba. Finally a rugged descent leads directly to the ferry-port of Puerto de las Nieves, for an easy onward connection to Tenerife.

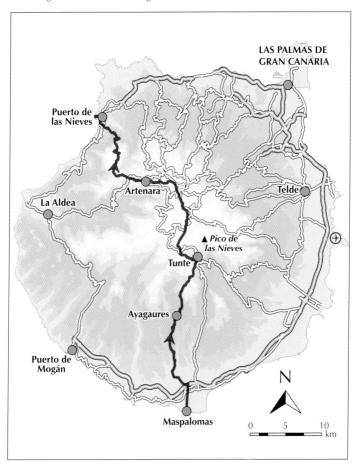

123

Some thought needs to be given to accommodation on this section as options are limited: you may wish to arrange taxi pick-ups in order to avail of facilities in one of the bigger towns or villages. Note that if you intend to use the campsite at Tamadaba, you need a permit, which can be applied for online but must be collected in person in Las Palmas.

TRANSPORT

Global bus services offer rapid access from the ferry-port at Las Palmas to the start of the trek at Maspalomas. There is no bus service to Ayagaures at the end of the first stage, though taxi pick-ups can be arranged. Global buses serve Tunte, Cruz Grande, Cruz de Tejeda and Artenara in the mountains, if you need to leave or join the route at those points. Global buses also serve the ferry-port of Puerto de las Nieves. Check the website for full details of services, www.guaguasglobal.com, or tel 928 939 316.

TOURIST INFORMATION

The main tourism website for Gran Canaria is www.grancanaria.com. Tourist information offices are located around the island, but the main ones for visiting trekkers are as follows:
- Airport, tel 928 574 117
- Las Palmas, Santa Catalina, tel 928 912 644
- Playa del Inglés, tel 928 771 550
- Cruz de Tejeda, tel 928 666 334
- Artenara, tel 928 666 102
- Puerto de las Nieves, tel 928 554 382

STAGE 15

Faro de Maspalomas to Ayagaures

Start	Faro de Maspalomas
Finish	Ayagaures
Distance	18km (11¼ miles)
Total ascent	530m (1740ft)
Total descent	220m (720ft)
Time	5hr 30min
Terrain	Mostly easy walking along level paths, followed by level roads and steep mountain roads.
Refreshments	Plenty of choice around Maspalomas. Bars at the Racing Kart, Montaña La Data and Ayagaures.
Transport	Plenty of buses serve Maspalomas, with the express services from Las Palmas being Global buses 30 and 50, and the one from the airport being Global bus 66. Global bus 5 links Las Palmas, the airport and Maspalomas. Global bus 70 serves Aqualand from Maspalomas. If a taxi is likely to be needed from Ayagaures, speak to a driver before leaving Maspalomas and take their number.
Accommodation	Plenty around Maspalomas, but very limited in Ayagaures.

Again, remember that there is no GR131 trail through Gran Canaria, so other signposted and waymarked trails are followed, starting with the S-54 from Maspalomas. Once clear of the busy and sprawling resort, the old PR GC 40 trail is followed along a mountain road, through the village of Montaña La Data, to the village of Ayagaures. Bear in mind that facilities at the finish are very limited so you may wish to arrange a taxi pick-up to return to Maspalomas.

Start at the landmark lighthouse of **Faro de Maspalomas**, only a short walk from a small bus station. Face the sea at **Playa de Maspalomas** and simply turn left to follow a coastal path which is surfaced in a variety of ways. While it is tempting to follow the sandy beach past the desert-like **Dunas de Maspalomas**, head inland from the Hotel Riu Palace Oasis. A path runs alongside the brackish water

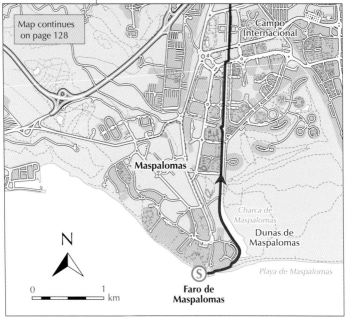

Map continues on page 128

Campo Internacional

Maspalomas

Charca de Maspalomas

Dunas de Maspalomas

Playa de Maspalomas

N

0   1
km

Ⓢ

Faro de Maspalomas

lagoon of **Charca de Maspalomas**, and a paved road continues onwards. Look to the right to spot a business offering camel rides, then walk straight past a bridge.

A brick-paved path passes the Charca de Maspalomas

A long, straight, broad and normally dry riverbed called the Barranco de Fataga is followed straight northwards, with mountains rising beyond, and there is a broad path on its left-hand side. Pass the stoutly fenced Parque Tony Gallardo, a botanical garden, then a roundabout beside a fenced resort. Continue past a curiously located ATM that is clearly only for the use of pedestrians. A restaurant stands beside a road bridge, and it is worth noting that there is a supermarket away to the left. However, keep following the broad riverside path, crossing a footbridge where a lesser riverbed joins from the left.

Pass, but do not cross, another footbridge on the way through the suburbs, and pass a small park before reaching a busy road bridge at **Campo Internacional**. Cross the road first, then turn right to cross the bridge, and follow the other riverside path further inland as signposted for the S-54 trail. Pass two footbridges and reach a roundabout and another signpost. A path leads beneath a busy, graffiti-splattered road bridge, then keep left at a fork where the riverbed is broad and vegetated.

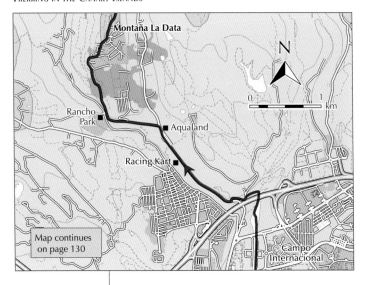

Map continues
on page 130

The S-54 trail is signposted straight ahead for Tunte and could be used as an alternative route, but this would miss Stage 16, which is a finer approach.

The path joins a dirt road where a signpost points right. Walk beneath a busy motorway bridge and turn left at a junction. ◄ The dirt road joins a tarmac road, where another left turn leads to a junction with a busier road. Turn right to continue, and it is best to keep to the left-hand side of the road to avoid the traffic. Pass the **Racing Kart** attraction and its snack bar. Further along the road, you reach bus shelters and a taxi stand at the **Aqualand** water park.

Next you reach a road junction where there might still be an old signpost for the PR GC 40 trail, which is curiously signposted for Llanos del Garañón – actually three days ahead along the trail. Turn left at the junction and keep straight ahead at another junction. When you reach the crossroads above **Rancho Park**, where camels are stabled, keep right to follow a road that climbs from the valley to the village of **Montaña La Data**. Simply follow the winding road up through the village, noting that there are a couple of bar-restaurants and a shop. The higher parts of the village are around 250m (820ft).

Although this is a road-walk, the road sits on the mountain crest for a short way, with steep drops on either side. It then keeps to the left of the mountainside ahead, around 310m (1015ft), then crosses a dip as it passes the failed housing development of **Monte León**. Pass a roundabout and the entrance to the Finca Justus Frantz, then keep left at a junction to follow the winding road further uphill. The route passes junctions where other roads are named after classical musicians, but always stay on the main mountain road, as all other roads lead only to dead ends among isolated houses.

Pass **Villa Vista Mar** and the road becomes very bendy, crossing a steep and rugged slope overlooking a valley. At the end of the valley is the popular attraction of **Palmitos Park**, but this zoo and botanical garden cannot be approached from the mountain road. Shortly after passing above the park, the road reaches its highest point of 490m (1605ft) at **Cima Pedro González**. ▸

The road is very convoluted as it descends, but avoid the temptation to short-cut as the mountainside is far

A road-walk links the villages of Montaña La Data and Ayagaures

There are splendid views of the village of Ayagaures, its reservoir and the mountains beyond.

129

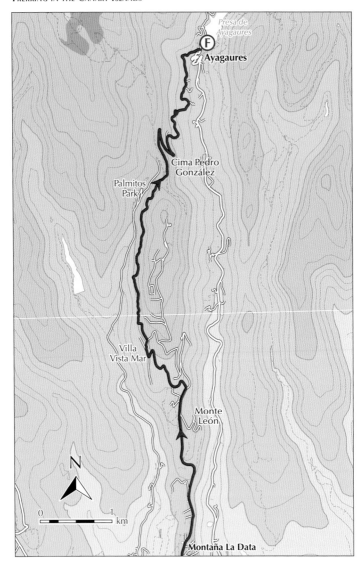

too rugged. Eventually, the road enters the little village of **Ayagaures**, around 310m (1015ft). There are no bus services, and the Pilancones de Ayagaures Bar is the only place offering food and drink. It might be necessary to arrange a taxi pick-up and return to Maspalomas, if accommodation can't be secured.

View of Ayagaures from the road at Cima Pedro González

STAGE 16
Ayagaures to Tunte

Start	Ayagaures
Finish	Church, Tunte
Distance	12.5km (7¾ miles)
Total ascent	900m (2950ft)
Total descent	320m (1050ft)
Time	4hr
Terrain	Easy road-walking at the start and finish. A steady climb up a stony path on a forested slope and a descent along a rugged track.
Refreshments	Bar at Ayagaures. Plenty of choice at Tunte.
Transport	None to Ayagaures, though taxis are available from Maspalomas. Global bus 18 links Tunte with Maspalomas and Tejeda. Global bus 34 links Tunte with Doctoral.
Accommodation	Very limited in Ayagaures but a little more at Tunte.

This stage follows an old mule path between Ayagaures and Tunte, now signposted as the S-57. The trail crosses a reservoir dam, climbs into pine forest and passes through a gap in the mountains. The forest was once home to a towering 550-year-old pine tree, Pino de Pilancones, sadly toppled in 2008. The descent leads to the village of Tunte, also referred to as San Bartolomé de Tirajana.

Starting from the little church and bar in **Ayagaures**, follow the road to the nearby dam of **Presa de Ayagaures**. A signpost for the S-57 points the way to Tunte, along a winding tarmac road that later becomes a dirt road. Cross the dam of another reservoir, **Presa de Gambuesa**, and continue along a road that is mostly broken concrete as it climbs past a few houses, palm trees and orchards. There are yellow paint marks, marker posts and a signpost that eventually points the way to a stone-paved path. ◄

Look back at the houses, with the reservoirs below and mountains on all sides.

The path climbs steadily from **Hoya Grande**, stone-paved or just stony. Pines grow among the scrub and

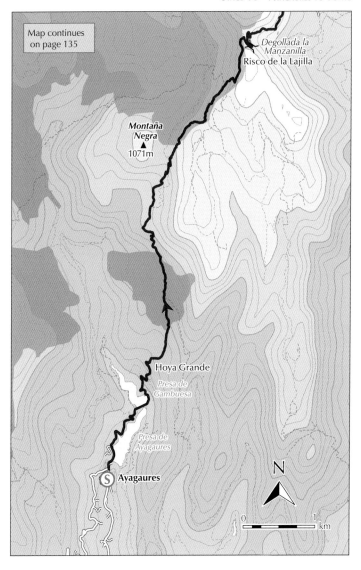

Map continues
on page 135

Degollada la
Manzanilla
Risco de la Lajilla

*Montaña
Negra*
▲
1071m

Hoya Grande
*Presa de
Gambuesa*

*Presa de
Ayagaures*

Ⓢ Ayagaures

N

0   1 km

133

Looking back from Hoya Grande to the reservoirs and Ayagaures

The extensive Parque Natural de Pilancones features mountainsides covered in dry pine forest and scrub.

A descent led to the enormous ancient pine of Pino de Pilancones, which stood from 1458 to 2008.

increase in number. There have clearly been forest fires in recent years and the forest has regenerated. Cistus is common in the ground scrub. As height is gained, the forest becomes a little denser, then it thins out, giving way to rugged, scrubby slopes. There are fine views while turning a corner above 800m (2540ft), and the ascent is gentler for a while. ◄ Cross a gully containing a dam and climb alongside another gully containing several dams. Pines reappear, but are sparser as the path reaches a signpost. Turn left along a track, as if heading for **Montaña Negra**, but when you reach another signpost, turn right up another path, passing above a concrete water store.

Cliffs and boulders loom ahead, but the path passes these easily. Views in all directions include pine-covered slopes with no habitations. Pass another cliff at **Risco de la Lajilla**, above 1000m (3280ft). A signpost stands where a once-popular path has been closed. ◄ Climb past bushy scrub to reach a signpost and a dirt road. Turn left up the dirt road, passing a water tap to reach a junction on the gap of **Degollada la Manzanilla**, at 1187m (3894ft), where there are signposts.

Turn sharp right to go down an old track that once carried vehicles, but suffered too many rock-falls, so it is now just a broad path. ▶ Note the stout stone buttresses that hold the track onto the mountainside. Wind downhill, passing a water trough beneath cliffs below **Morro de las Vacas**. The cliffs feature towers of rock, or overhang dramatically where the track has been cut into a soft, cream-coloured layer of rock. Turn a corner and later cross a scree slope. Generally, pines grow above the track and almonds grow below it. Pass a fenced field at **Llano Pelado**, then join and follow a concrete road downhill from a farm at 998m (3274ft).

Further downhill, keep left along a tarmac road then turn right at a signposted junction at **Huerta del Conde**. Turn left along a main road to pass the access road for the Hotel las Tirajanas. Keep straight ahead at another junction to walk down Calle El Roque. Turn right down the brick-paved Calle San Juan, then later turn left along Calle Corazón Jesús, and turn right down Calle Padre Claret.

If you have no wish to descend to Tunte, continue straight ahead along the forest road to Cruz Grande.

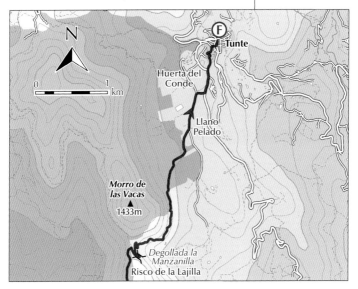

The descent to Tunte follows a rugged path

Turn left at the bottom to follow Calle Reyes Católicos through the centre of **Tunte**, around 890m (2920ft). The church, which is dedicated to the Apostle St James, or Santiago, is almost hidden behind two big pine trees.

TUNTE

The ancient mountain town of Tunte is also known as San Bartolomé de Tirajana. The surrounding area features pine forest and cultivation terraces, while the cliffs of Risco de San Bartolomé rise to the highest point on Gran Canaria – Pico de las Nieves. The town has a church dedicated to San Bartolomé, as well as one dedicated to the Apostle St James, or Santiago. Observant walkers might already have spotted 'Camino de Santiago' signposts and there is a recognised pilgrim trail stretching across Gran Canaria from Playa del Inglés to Gáldar. The pilgrim trail follows our own route from Ayagaures to Tunte, and onwards beyond Cruz de Tejeda to Moriscos.

STAGE 17

Tunte to Cruz de Tejeda

Start	Church, Tunte
Finish	Cruz de Tejeda
Distance	15.5km (9½ miles)
Total ascent	1020m (3345ft)
Total descent	400m (1310ft)
Time	5hr 30min
Terrain	Paths vary from stone-paved to stony, through forest or across bare rock, and are sometimes steep. Towards the end the paths run high, but parallel to roads.
Refreshments	Plenty of choice at Tunte. Hotel bar-restaurants at Cruz de Tejeda.
Transport	Global bus 18 links Tunte with Maspalomas, Cruz Grande and Tejeda, below Cruz de Tejeda. Global bus 305 serves Cruz de Tejeda from Tejeda and San Mateo.
Accommodation	Hotels at Tunte and Cruz de Tejeda.

Leaving Tunte, a path climbs through pine forest towards the high mountains. An exceptional stone-paved path negotiates overhanging cliffs, then more pine forest is encountered over the highest point on the route through Gran Canaria. The 'Cumbre', or the high crest of the island, features paths that often run parallel to roads towards the strategic gap of Cruz de Tejeda.

Leave the church of Santiago in **Tunte** and walk up Calle Reyes Católicos. Turn right as signposted for the S-50 for 'Cruz Grande' and 'Cruz Tejeda', up the brick-paved Calle Padre Claret. Turn left up Calle Corazón de Jesús and later turn right up Calle San Juan. Walk straight up this street, reaching a road junction near a cemetery with a fine entrance. Go down to a nearby crossroads and go straight through, as if heading for the Bodegas Las Tirajanas. You reach a signposted junction, where a track is marked as the Camino de Santiago. Follow this and later continue straight ahead up a stone-paved path through pine forest.

There are stony and rocky parts, but the way is mostly stone-paved with occasional steps. The path zigzags uphill, then levels out at times and even descends gently at **El Andén Blanco**, with fine views where there are gaps in the forest. Climb to a track and follow it up to

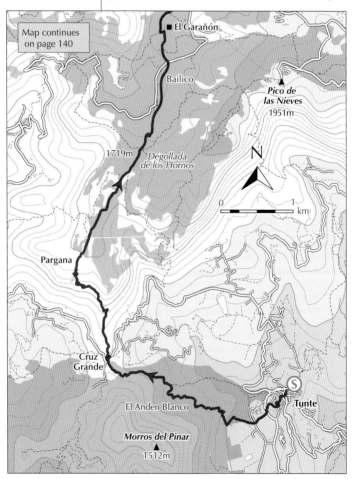

Map continues on page 140

El Garañón

Bailico

Pico de las Nieves 1951m

1719m

Degollada de los Hornos

N

0   1 km

Pargana

Cruz Grande

S

Tunte

El Anden Blanco

Morros del Pinar 1512m

a road at **Cruz Grande**, at 1215m (3986ft), where there is a rocky cutting. ▶ Turn right along the road, then left as signposted up a concrete road. This becomes stone-paved as it approaches a house. Pass the house to follow a rocky path uphill, noting the wonderfully varied scrub and its fine fragrances. The path is partly stone-paved as it works its way up to a crest for splendid all-round views.

There are occasional Global bus 18 services.

▶ Later, cross an almond terrace on a level path and then start climbing. The path is stone-paved as it zigzags up a rugged cliff face, passing beneath overhanging rock. The amazing thing is that the path climbs with relative ease and is excellently engineered throughout. Climb past a small reservoir and a stand of pines, then zigzag further up a rocky slope at **Pargana**, where very little grows.

Look carefully at the awesome cliffs ahead and try to spot a path.

The stone paving ends on bare rock, so watch carefully where the rock has been worn by walkers heading towards a pine forest. The path gradually makes its way up through the forest, but also crosses rocky areas. ▶ The main path gradually rises, reaching the gap of **Degollada de los Hornos**, at 1719m (5640ft), where signposted paths cross. This is one of the highest points on the trail through Gran Canaria.

A short path to the left is signposted for Ventana del Nublo, catching a glimpse of Roque Nublo from a crest at 1688m (5538ft), as well as a nearby rock arch.

Looking down on a little reservoir perched high above Cruz Grande

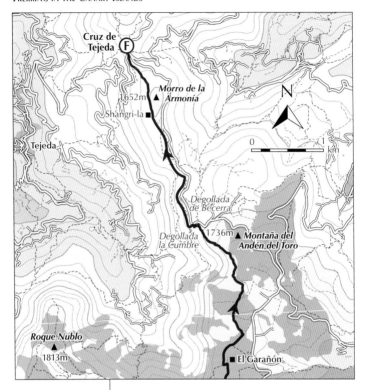

The highest point on Gran Canaria is **Pico de las Nieves**, which rises to 1951m (6401ft) and lies 3km (2 miles) away, roughly north-east. Although it can be approached by using a well-forested path with occasional views, marked as the S-51, the summit itself is occupied by a military installation and is out of bounds to visitors. Although *nieve* means 'snow', it rarely snows, even at this altitude.

Go straight ahead down a path, crossing an area of bare rock in the forest. Step over a stream to follow a broad forest path almost to a road. Don't follow the road, but turn right and walk roughly parallel to it, passing a basic campground at **Bailico**. Later, the path crosses a couple of streams, if they are flowing, then it climbs a little and crosses the road. ▶

Watch carefully to catch the first glimpse of the distant pyramidal peak of El Teide on Tenerife.

The path becomes a track flanked by fences, leading to **El Garañón**, around 1670m (5480ft). A number of cabins offer 'accommodation and sporting activities in the natural environment'. Turn left to join a broad dirt road then turn right as signposted along it, through less forested terrain. When you reach a pool, there is a path signposted to the left. Follow it gently up through a small valley among pines. Cross a dirt road and the path is rather vague as it climbs through forest to cross a track at a signpost. The path is partly stone-paved as it descends, passing below a water store. ▶

Fine views take in some of Gran Canaria's most notable summits, as well as the distant El Teide on Tenerife.

The path roughly contours across a slope that was badly burnt in 2017. Descend from **Montaña del Andén del Toro**, almost touching a road bend at **Degollada la Cumbre**, at 1570m (5150ft). The path passes a white house and later reaches another road bend at **Degollada de Becerra**, at 1552m (5092ft). A car park and viewpoint are located here, and there might also be a souvenir stall offering taste samples of Canarian produce. A stone-paved path runs parallel to the road, passing a house to reach another road bend. Continue through a burnt forest, where the path leads onto a dirt road. The dirt road leads to a secluded property called **Shangri-la**, at almost 1600m (5250ft), from where a path continues and offers fine views. A fairly rugged descent leads to the road at the gap of **Cruz de Tejeda**, at 1512m (4960ft).

CRUZ DE TEJEDA

Despite being on a high gap in the mountains, Cruz de Tejeda offers a surprising range of facilities. There are two hotels – El Refugio and the Parador de Cruz de Tejeda – as well as a number of Canarian produce and souvenir stalls that operate during the day. Occasional buses cross the gap, which could prove useful if accommodation can't be secured at this point. Information about the Camino de Santiago, which has been followed for the past two stages, can be obtained from the reception area of El Refugio.

STAGE 18
Cruz de Tejeda to Tamadaba

Start	Cruz de Tejeda
Finish	Área Recreativa de Tamadaba
Distance	17.5km (11 miles)
Total ascent	750m (2460ft)
Total descent	1060m (3475ft)
Time	5hr 30min
Terrain	Mountainside paths, forest paths and tracks, as well as some road-walking. Some ascents and descents are steep and rugged.
Refreshments	Plenty of choice in Artenara. None at Tamadaba.
Transport	Global bus 305 serves Cruz de Tejeda from Tejeda and San Mateo. Global bus 220 serves Artenara from Teror, passing the viewpoint of Degollada de las Palomas.
Accommodation	Two hotels at Cruz de Tejeda, limited choice in Artenara, basic campsite at Tamadaba.

This stage needs some thought as accommodation is sparse. Either walk the short distance from Cruz de Tejeda to Artenara, where there is limited accommodation, and finish with a long walk the following day, or walk to Tamadaba and camp in the forest, finishing with a short walk the following day. The route is largely through pine-forested mountains, but there are good views in many places. Bear in mind that this entire stage suffered a devastating fire in the summer of 2019.

Leave **Cruz de Tejeda** by following the road that leads to a car park behind the Parador hotel. Two paths leave this car park, so take the one that lies furthest left, which climbs and passes to the left-hand side of a small reservoir wall. Keep climbing and zigzagging up a slope of pines, then there are splendid views as the path basically contours across the steep slopes of **Monte Constantino**. ◄

The path passes a prominent rock tower and later descends to a road on a gap at **Degollada de las Palomas**, at 1623m (5325ft). This is a fine viewpoint in good

The towers of Roque Nublo and Roque Bentayga are seen, with El Teide far beyond Moriscos.

weather and there is a shelter in case of rain. A path, signposted as the S-90, leaves the road, climbing steps onto a bushy slope, then entering pine forest. Later, the path becomes a track, reaching a place where the S-90 trail is signposted left. Continue to a junction on a forested crest and keep straight ahead, following a path that roughly contours across the steep southern face of **Moriscos**. The path must be about 1730m (5675ft) high, which would make it the highest point reached on the way across Gran Canaria.

Rock towers on the steep slopes of Monte Constantino

Eventually, the path descends to a track, where there is a notice about the **Cuevas de Caballero**, at 1620m (5315ft). This site can be explored, with care, by turning left and crossing an awkward rocky slope. The caves were once inhabited by aboriginal Canarii and are now protected by railings and locked gates. Views across the valley are splendid. Follow the forest track downhill until you reach a three-way signpost where you turn left along a path. This zigzags down a forested slope and passes a bend on the more circuitous track. Continue downhill, passing a path junction to return to the track, then turn left to continue along the track.

Eventually, you reach a signpost at a junction on a bend. Another cave, **Cueva de los Candiles** is signposted off-route, but if you're not inclined to visit, then keep straight ahead and follow the track to another signposted junction at 1417m (4649ft). Carry on straight ahead and reach yet another signpost, where a path on the right descends and cuts out a lengthy bend from the track. Continue a little further down the track, then go down stone steps on the right, following a rather worn, bendy path down past more signposts to reach a track, road and map-board at **La Degollada**, at 1305m (4280ft).

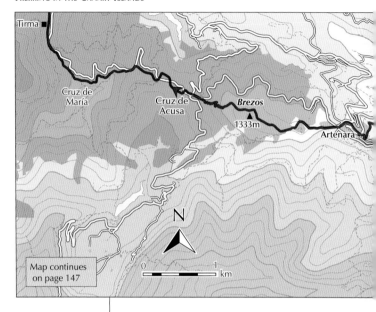

Map continues
on page 147

Follow a track across a slope. Later it gives way to concrete, descending to a bend where the viewpoint of Mirador de los Poetas is located. This offers good views of Artenara and its surrounding countryside and forests, as well as featuring poems mounted on plaques. The concrete road gives way to tarmac on a winding descent into **Artenara**, around 1230m (4035ft).

ARTENARA

Explore this attractive village, which is the highest and one of the oldest settlements in Gran Canaria. The village was evacuated during the forest fires of 2019. There are some splendid viewpoints and a wonderful cliff-side balcony, as well as offers of food and drink. Accommodation is very limited, but includes some intriguing cave houses. If staying in the village bear in mind that only 7km (4½ miles) have been covered, and the shortfall in distance must be added to the following day's walk. There are occasional buses, if leaving the route, and taxis are also available if required.

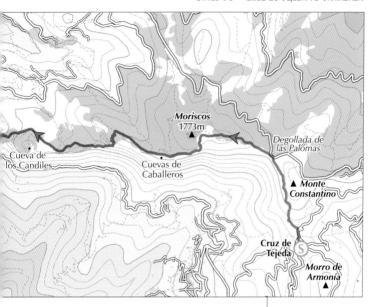

Leave the village by walking down the main road to reach a roundabout and signposts. Go straight through to the other side and walk up a steep road, passing the Mirador de Las Cañaditas. Pass some large buildings at La Atalya to reach a signposted junction near a helipad and turn left. You'll come to another junction where there are map-boards and a signpost. ▶ There are two tracks, one leading downhill and one leading uphill. Take the uphill track, which soon runs at a gentler gradient along a forested crest, then there is a slight dip as you pass a mast. Soon afterwards, when you come to the end of the track, a path heads left.

Walking routes abound on these forested slopes, leading in all directions.

The path traverses the fire-ravaged slopes of **Brezos**, touching 1300m (4265ft), then it descends through the forest using stone steps and zigzags. When you come to a road, either follow the signposts exactly, or simply turn left to reach a nearby crossroads at 1099m (3606ft) and continue straight ahead, walking parallel to the road.

145

A fine path on the slopes of Altavista on the way to Tamadaba

Cross the slopes of **Cruz de Acusa**, then cross the road and follow a short path to a three-way signpost. Cross the road again and follow the path up 16 stone steps. The path appears to run parallel to the road, but as it climbs it also short-cuts a lengthy bend in the road before joining it again.

Turn left up the road until you reach a viewpoint, signpost and map-board. Walk up stone steps and the path later reaches a three-way signpost. ◄ Keep right and traverse the forested slopes, passing a spring and later descending past a viewpoint. When you come to a junction, go either way as both paths soon re-join. Descend to the road and follow it past a forestry house at **Tirma**, at 1172m (3845ft). ◄

Left leads to the summit of Altavista and the distant town of Aldea de San Nicolás.

The house and forest suffered damage during the fires of 2019.

At the next three-way signpost a path on the left runs parallel to the road, later passing another signpost in a dip near the road. The path and the road part company, passing round opposite sides of a forested hill. Follow the path, which joins a track and quickly reaches a road junction at 1222m (4009ft). Keep straight ahead as signposted, following the bendy road until another signpost indicates a path on the left. This path passes a three-way signpost on a forested slope, then soon crosses the road and runs below it for a change, through forest at **Pinar de Tamadaba**.

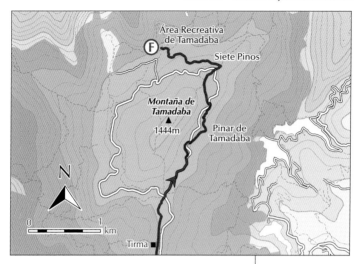

Later, the path crosses back over the road and climbs to a broad, forested gap on **Montaña de Tamadaba**, where there is a path intersection at 1321m (4334ft). Turn right and the path soon begins to descend, crossing the road yet again. Walk straight downhill until a signpost indicates a left turn, then a gradually descending traverse leads across forested slopes at **Siete Pinos**. A signpost is reached at 1202m (3944ft), where the route turns right. However, those intending to camp for the night at a forest campsite should turn left.

ÁREA RECREATIVA DE TAMADABA

The campsite, toilets and map-boards are only a short walk off-route. Note that it can be misty and damp in this area, and the pine trees can drip continuously in those conditions. Great skeins of lichen hang from the branches of the trees. Camping is free, but you need a permit which must be applied for in advance through the Cabildo de Gran Canaria website. Be warned that the process is time-consuming and inconvenient, as you will be required to collect the permit in person in Las Palmas. See https://cabildo. grancanaria.com/formulario-solicitud-permiso-acampadas.

STAGE 19
Tamadaba to Puerto de las Nieves

Start	Área Recreativa de Tamadaba
Finish	Harbour, Puerto de las Nieves
Distance	10.5km (6½ miles)
Total ascent	50m (165ft)
Total descent	1250m (4100ft)
Time	3hr 30min
Terrain	Forest tracks and paths give way to a steep and rugged descent on a mountain path, followed by a traverse across a steep slope. Towards the end a mixture of tracks and paths give way to a road-walk into a ferry-port.
Refreshments	Plenty of choice at Puerto de las Nieves.
Transport	Global bus 103 serves Puerto de las Nieves from Las Palmas, while Global bus 101 serves Puerto de las Nieves from Aldea de San Nicolás. Puerto de las Nieves has daily ferry services to Santa Cruz de Tenerife.
Accommodation	Forest campsite at Tamadaba, more choice in Puerto de las Nieves.

The final stage of the trek across Gran Canaria sees a sustained descent from the forested uplands of Tamadaba onto increasingly arid slopes that were once pressed into agricultural use. Steep slopes of stone-strewn scrub remain, served by old paths and tracks. If you reach Puerto de las Nieves early in the afternoon, there may be time to catch the ferry to Tenerife to continue along the GR131.

Leave the campsite at **Tamadaba** and walk back along the track. Keep straight ahead, passing the signpost that you passed at the end of the previous day. Continue on the track, going around the chain barrier, then later take a signposted stone-paved path on the left, which widens into a track. In one part of the forest the route crosses bare rock and comes to a junction where a marker indicates a route bearing a number 7. Follow this and a

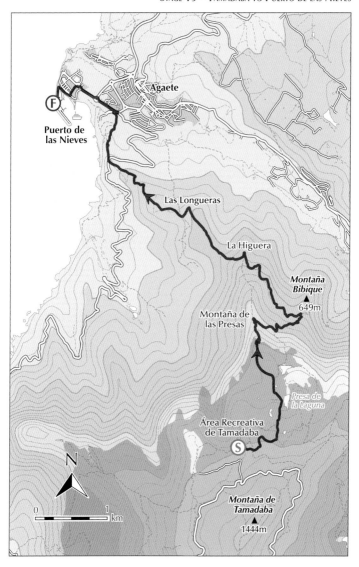

149

gentle descent leads to a track junction around 1050m (3445ft), where the reservoir of **Presa de la Laguna** lies to the right. However, keep straight ahead and continue the descent, reaching another junction where the way ahead is marked for San Pedro.

The path runs down across the slopes of **Montaña de las Presas**, eventually reaching noticeboards and the start of a rugged path, around 1020m (3345ft). Zigzag downhill and watch for a memorial cross, as shortly afterwards the path suddenly turns sharp right. The way is plain and obvious, but drops down a steep and rugged slope, eventually passing a pipe protruding from the ground. Reach a gap at 638m (2095ft) where there is a signpost and an *era*, or circular threshing floor. **Montaña Bibique** lies just beyond.

Turn left and follow a path that traverses a slope, crossing a stream beside a fig tree. The path later passes some old terraces, then the slope steepens, the path narrows and more care is necessary. After a descent and another traverse, there is a sharp left turn at **La Higuera** and you'll see a little shrine occupying a niche in a rock face. The path makes its way onto a broad ridge where

An era, *or threshing floor, seen on the descent from Tamadaba*

the descent continues more easily, and eventually it joins a track. This quickly reaches a gap around 360m (1180ft) where there is another *era*. ▶

The track makes sweeping zigzags while descending fairly gently on an arid slope of scrub. Watch out for places where a clear path offers short-cuts through the upper zigzags. However, the track has to be followed further downhill until the last big zigzag can be short-cut in order to descend directly to a road, around 170m (560ft). There is a nearby bend and traffic tends to move fast, so cross with care to reach a signpost that points along a broad path.

The descent is fairly direct, but the ground underfoot along the path is rugged in places. Eventually, the path runs into a stone-paved road, which quickly descends to a road junction, passing a final signpost and map-board. Turn left to follow the road towards **Puerto de las Nieves**, but note that there is a broad and safe path running along the right-hand side of the road. Pass a roundabout and follow the road to another roundabout, where there is a bus terminus and the Hotel Puerto de las Nieves.

Enjoy fine views of the rugged west coast of Gran Canaria.

PUERTO DE LAS NIEVES

This is a busy little port having a regular daily turnaround of ferries running to and from Tenerife. The town offers plenty of accommodation, food and drink. While the port looks modern it has a few features of historical interest, notably the little Ermita Nuestra Señora de las Nieves. The surrounding cliffs shelter the harbour on one side, while a stout breakwater protects it on the other. Look carefully to spot the stump of rock called Dedo de Dios, or 'God's Finger', though it is gradually wearing away.

If there is a chance of transferring straight onto a ferry for Tenerife, then turn left to leave the roundabout and follow Calle Antón Cerezo. Turn left at the end of the street, then turn immediately right across a pedestrian crossing and go down a few steps. Turn right again to follow the narrow pedestrianised Paseo de los Poetas past numerous bars and restaurants. At the end, turn left to walk to the ferry-port and catch the next available ferry to Tenerife.

The final descent to Puerto de las Nieves for the ferry to Tenerife

GRAN CANARIA TO TENERIFE

The trek through Gran Canaria finishes very conveniently at Puerto de las Nieves, where regular daily Fred Olsen ferries offer crossings to Santa Cruz de Tenerife, taking 1hr 20min. Naviera Armas ferries don't operate on this route, but take a much longer time to sail between Las Palmas and Santa Cruz.

Advance planning is necessary to ensure a successful continuation along the GR131. On Tenerife, the GR131 doesn't run coast to coast, as it does on other islands, but starts and finishes at altitude, some distance inland. On arrival at Santa Cruz, walk from the ferry-port to the big TITSA bus station. There are two choices at this point. Either catch one of the regular buses to La Laguna, taking only 15–20 minutes, or catch a tram, or *tranvía*, which is the only opportunity to travel by rail anywhere in the Canary Islands. Join the tram outside the bus station and get off at the 'intercambiador' stop at La Laguna, which is beside the bus station.

The final part of the journey involves catching a bus from La Laguna to La Esperanza. Although TITSA buses appear to have a monopoly on Tenerife, the bus company Transportes La Esperanza operates bus 41 between La Laguna and La Esperanza. Taxis could also be used to speed up the transfer. The first stage of the GR131 on Tenerife is long and very remote, as well as completely lacking any kind of services. Have a good plan sorted out well in advance.

Fred Olsen, tel 902 100 107 www.fredolsen.es

TENERIFE

Looking down through pine forest towards Roque del Conde and Roque Imoque (Stage 24)

TENERIFE
93.5km (58 miles) 5 days

The GR131 runs coast to coast across most of the Canary Islands, but on Tenerife it starts and finishes far inland, at considerable altitude. Technically, the route is unfinished, as it was planned to run from the Anaga peninsula, past La Laguna, and over the mountainous 'Cumbre' to finish in Arona. The first stages haven't been developed and for many years the route has run only from La Esperanza to Arona. Despite that, the variety of terrain is impressive, and the route runs consistently higher than any of the routes across the other islands.

The first stage, from La Esperanza to La Caldera, needs careful planning. It is long and almost entirely forested, with no facilities of any kind from start to finish. It should be possible to start at first light, then keep up a steady pace with an eye on the time, in order to finish before the last bus descends from La Caldera. On the next stage, accommodation remains a problem, as there is none from start to finish. Even on the third stage, the only accommodation is the expensive Parador de Cañadas del Teide, and camping in the national park is not

A short signposted path leads towards the Parador

only forbidden, but park staff will challenge anyone found pitching a tent. On the other hand, some trekkers are really very good at staying out of sight and camping very discreetly!

The highest point on the trail is reached on the shoulder of the mighty mountain of Guajara, around 2420m (7940ft). However, those with stamina might prefer to take the opportunity to vary the route and include a summit bid on the enormous El Teide, whose summit reaches 3718m (12,198ft). A detailed route description is provided.

The descent passes through Vilaflor, reputed to be the highest Spanish village, before the finish is reached in Arona. A simple bus ride down to Los Cristianos would hopefully link neatly with the next available ferry to La Gomera. If not, then Los Cristianos offers plenty of accommodation and the journey could continue with an early morning ferry the following day.

TRANSPORT

TITSA bus services offer rapid access from the ferry-port at Santa Cruz to the university town of La Laguna.

Transportes La Esperanza buses run from La Laguna to the start of the trek at La Esperanza. TITSA buses are available at the end of each stage of the GR131, but they are very limited on the highest part of the trail and it is as well to book seats in advance if relying on them to join or leave the trail in the national park. TITSA buses also run from Arona, at the end of the trail, down to the ferry-port of Los Cristianos. Check the website for full details of services, www.titsa.com, or tel 922 531 300.

TOURIST INFORMATION

The main tourism website for Tenerife is www.webtenerife.com. Tourist information offices are located around the island, but the main ones for visiting trekkers are as follows:

- Airport (Norte), tel 922 255 433
- Airport (Sur), tel 922 392 037
- Santa Cruz, tel 922 892 903
- La Laguna, tel 922 631 194
- La Orotava, tel 922 324 367
- Puerto de la Cruz, tel 922 384 769
- Vilaflor, tel 922 709 002
- Los Cristianos, tel 922 757 130

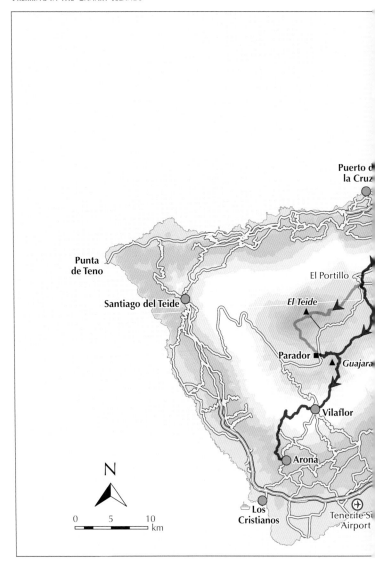

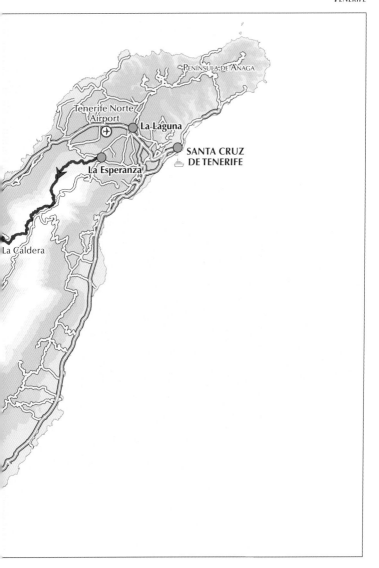

STAGE 20
La Esperanza to La Caldera

Start	Plaza del Ayuntamiento, La Esperanza
Finish	Bus stop, La Caldera
Distance	29.5km (18¼ miles)
Total ascent	1650m (5415ft)
Total descent	1360m (4460ft)
Time	10hr
Terrain	Mostly forested slopes criss-crossed by dirt roads, tracks and paths. There are several ascents and descents, sometimes featuring flights of steps and sometimes steep and rugged.
Refreshments	Bar-restaurants at La Esperanza. Bar-restaurant at La Caldera.
Transport	Transportes La Esperanza bus 41 links La Laguna with La Esperanza. TITSA bus 345 links La Caldera with La Orotava and Puerto de la Cruz.
Accommodation	Limited at La Esperanza and none at La Caldera (a regular bus service allows access to options elsewhere).

This is a very long stage and there are no easy ways to shorten it. However, much of the walking is easy, along forest tracks and paths that are only occasionally steep. Over 1000 log steps climb and descend during this stage, as well as 100 more stone steps. Start at first light from La Esperanza and keep track of progress to be sure to catch one of the last buses from La Caldera. Alternatively, arrange a pick-up where the route runs close to the road on the 'Cumbre', or camp discreetly somewhere.

If starting very early in the morning, there might be one or two bar-restaurants open.

Start in the middle of **La Esperanza**, around 900m (2950ft), on the spacious Plaza del Ayuntamiento. ◀ Go up a road signposted for the post office, or *correos*, to find another little plaza and a *sendero* signpost for the Camino Natural de Anaga-Chasna. Stone steps climb from the top of the plaza into a well-wooded valley.

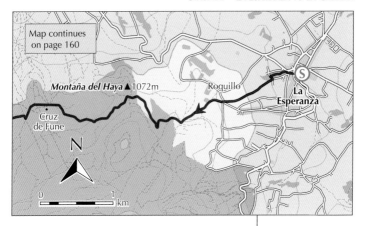

Map continues on page 160

Montaña del Haya ▲ 1072m   Roquillo   La Esperanza

Cruz de Fune

N

0   1 km

Watch for red/white paint marks, which indicate more steps and a footbridge. Cross this, but don't cross the next footbridge, keeping to the left-hand side of the valley. The path climbs and joins a road.

Turn left to reach a signposted road junction, then turn right to climb steeply out of the town. ▸ When you come to a roundabout at **Roquillo**, at a junction of five roads, simply continue straight uphill. The road reaches a green house and gives way to a dirt road entering a forest. There are heather trees, tall eucalyptus and occasional stout pines. Avoid all turnings until a GR131 signpost points right, around 1100m (3610ft). Walk down a track that drops gently from the dirt road. There are essentially two types of forest here – a dense laurisilva forest and a tall pine forest. Wind downhill to reach another junction near the forested hump of **Montaña del Haya** and turn left.

Markers and a signpost show the way down to a junction and a little shrine at **Cruz de Fune**, at just over 1000m (3280ft). Keep straight ahead and join a dirt road, turning left. Soon afterwards, turn right then almost immediately turn left along Pista Las Agulillas. The trees in the forest are shorter for a while, then become taller again. The dirt road undulates gently and might be used by occasional vehicles and cyclists, as well as walkers.

Catch a glimpse of Santa Cruz to the left, with Gran Canaria far beyond.

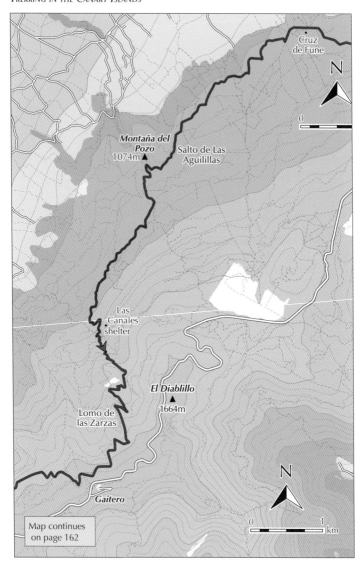

Cruz de Fune

Montaña del Pozo
1074m ▲

Salto de Las Aguilillas

Las Canales shelter

El Diablillo
1664m ▲

Lomo de las Zarzas

Gaitero

Map continues on page 162

0 1 km

Although marked as the GR131, there are other signposts and markers for shorter trails in the area. The dirt road generally rises to pass **Salto de Las Aguilillas**. A signpost on a bend is immediately followed by a left turn up a path through dense forest. Climb log steps, followed by some stretches where bare rock is exposed.

Cross a dirt road and climb to reach another dirt road, turning right to follow it. Pass a junction and go round a bend, then look ahead to catch a glimpse of the summit of El Teide. ▶ Keep following the dirt road as is winds and climbs, reaching a **shelter** and a water tap at **Las Canales**, around 1250m (4100ft).

There is also a brief view down to Puerto de la Cruz, but only because of a gap cut through the forest to accommodate a power line.

The GR131 runs through extensive pine forests throughout the day

Walk up to a signposted junction and turn left up a track, then almost immediately turn right up a path. This climbs and crosses a track, then climbs further and crosses another track. The laurisilva forest becomes sparse, but there are always heather trees among the tall pines, and you'll also see tough broom in some places. After a convoluted stretch the path joins a track. Turn left along it, then turn right and climb another path. After climbing **Lomo de las Zarzas**, the path bends round a valley and there is a glimpse down to the coast. As the path continues higher, there are several ascents involving log steps, varying from just a few to a few dozen each time. Some short flights also go down a little.

A short, steep climb would lead quickly to a road high on the 'Cumbre' near Gaitero, if you've arranged a pick-up from there.

The route crosses a track on a crest at over 1660m (5445ft), where there is a signpost. ◀ Take care to spot the path dropping from the track, which is initially obscured by broom. Flights of log steps now descend either a few at a time, or a few dozen at a time, crossing a dirt road on the way. There are short ascents as well as descents.

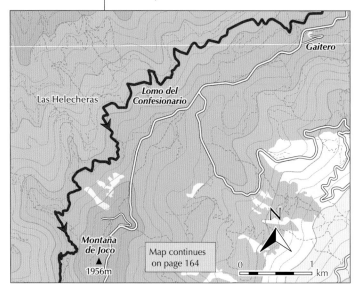

Las Helecheras

Lomo del Confesionario

Gaitero

Montaña de Joco
▲
1956m

Map continues on page 164

N

0   1
km

The path later runs parallel to a dirt road, crossing a steep slope while having stretches of fencing alongside for protection. All of a sudden, the path zigzags uphill with the aid of log steps, reaching a signpost at over 1550m (5085ft) on **Lomo del Confesionario**.

Massive boulders lie on a steep slope ahead and the path is fenced as it passes them. Ascents feature more log steps and two signposts are passed at **Las Helecheras**. There is a glimpse of El Teide before a few steps go downhill. ▶ Go down a few more log steps, then up a few, to join a dirt road. Turn right and follow it until another path is marked on the left, climbing above it. Flights of log steps continue to climb then the path crosses a track as indicated by a signpost. The pine forest thins out and a notice warns of the danger of rock-falls from the cliffs of **Montaña de Joco**, so walk with care.

There are stone steps and several stretches of fencing for protection, as well as a long section where the path cuts across a cliff-face that sprouts abundant houseleeks, around 1750m (5740ft). Stone steps zigzag downhill, then the path zigzags uphill to cross a little gap. Descend again in a sweeping zigzag, then the path continues more easily across the mountainside, eventually passing another warning sign for trekkers coming in the opposite direction. On reaching a non-GR signpost around 1580m (5185ft), a right turn leads down a rugged path, which becomes easier and passes a GR131 signpost.

Continue descending from **Roque del Topo** using old stone and log steps. ▶ The path crosses a junction of dirt roads and continues its descent, landing on another dirt road further downhill, around 1160m (3805ft). Turn left to follow the road onwards. It is very bendy and first crosses a bridge, passing the **Casa del Agua**, which was built for the abstraction of water. Later, the road crosses another bridge and passes a **shelter** at **Pero Gil**, where lots of walking routes are signposted. Yet another bridge is crossed as the dirt road finally reaches a tarmac road. Follow this past the crater of **La Caldera**, which is a recreational area around 1190m (3905ft). Pass a rustic bar-restaurant to reach a car park, signposts, map-board and bus stop.

There will be more opportunities to spot the mountain later in the day.

Note the skeins of lichen hanging from the trees; this area can hold cloud and mist that keeps the ground moist.

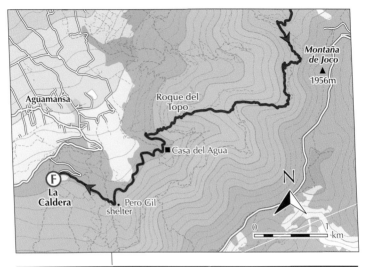

LA CALDERA

If the crater at La Caldera is smoking, it is only because everyone is cooking on barbecues! There is no accommodation here, and not even a campsite. Apart from the food and drink offered at the bar-restaurant, it is necessary to leave the route in search of all other services. A regular bus service descends to La Orotava (30min) and Puerto de la Cruz (1hr), which offer everything a weary trekker could desire, and the same bus allows an early start the following morning back at La Caldera.

The **Orotava valley** is so big that many visitors don't even realise they are in it. It was formed by a catastrophic landslide that sent a tsunami racing across the ocean. The steep slopes are fertile and support terraces of fruit and vegetables, while the upper slopes are covered in laurisilva and pine forest. These draw moisture from the clouds and drip water into the ground, which is then abstracted for agricultural and domestic use. La Orotava is a busy town located below several high villages, while the urban sprawl of Puerto de la Cruz lies close to the sea.

Rugged cliffs and buttresses rise above the forest near La Caldera

STAGE 21
La Caldera to El Portillo

Start	Bus stop, La Caldera
Finish	Restaurant, El Portillo
Distance	13.5km (8¼ miles)
Total ascent	1090m (3575ft)
Total descent	240m (790ft)
Time	5hr
Terrain	Mostly well-forested slopes bearing easy tracks and more rugged paths.
Refreshments	Bar-restaurant at La Caldera. Bar-restaurant at El Portillo.
Transport	TITSA bus 345 links Puerto de la Cruz and La Orotava with La Caldera. TITSA bus 348 links Puerto de la Cruz with El Portillo and the Parador de las Cañadas del Teide. TITSA bus 342 links El Portillo with the Parador de las Cañadas del Teide, Vilaflor, Arona and Los Cristianos.
Accommodation	None: La Orotava, Puerto de la Cruz and the Parador are all accessible by bus.

This stage starts among laurisilva forest and, apart from brief views of lower cultivated slopes, it climbs relentlessly through higher pine forests. On misty days the trees drip incessantly. Paths and tracks criss-cross the slopes, so it is wise to keep an eye on the GR131 signposts and markers. At the end of the day, the trail emerges from the forest and there are views into the amazing Teide National Park.

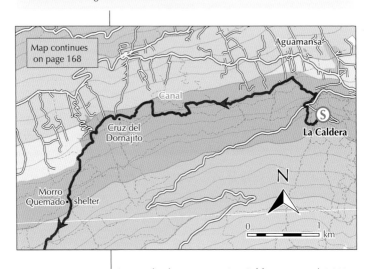

Leave the bus stop at **La Caldera**, around 1190m (3905ft), and walk the length of the car park to find a path signposted down a forested slope. This is laurisilva forest containing taller pines. There are a number of paths on the slope, so watch for red and white markers to stay on course. Go down steps and go through a tunnel beneath a main road. Cross a track and follow a path to a bend further down the track. Walk along the track until a signpost points right down a path, eventually reaching another track on the outskirts of the village of **Aguamansa**, around 1040m (3410ft).

Some areas have trees whose lower branches have been removed.

Turn left to follow the track past a couple of properties surrounded by tall fences and continue straight along a rugged path through woodland. ◄ Keep an eye open

to spot markers at junctions and pass another property surrounded by a tall fence. A signpost points left up a path, which leads to another track. Turn right to follow the track and pass an isolated house. Keep right at a track junction and almost immediately turn right down a path, as marked. Cross a stone-clad pipeline, the **Canal de Aguamansa**, and descend to a signpost around 1000m (3280ft). Turn left and the path later climbs a flight of log steps beside a concrete-walled reservoir, running close to the pipeline again.

Walkers follow a track through laurisilva forest above Aguamansa

Cross a track and go down log steps, again running close to the pipeline, and cross a road. A flight of log steps drops to a shelter and signposts at **Cruz del Dornajito**, around 1020m (3345ft). ▸ Climb a flight of log steps and follow the path past fields, then after a short walk along a concrete track, another path passes another field. After turning round a valley, the path becomes a track as it climbs to a junction beside another pipeline. Turn right and rise to a signpost and junction beside a huge pine tree.

The cross itself is hidden from sight in a cave, but it can be visited by going down a short path.

Keep left at this and other junctions to climb further. Go straight through a signposted track intersection on a wooded slope and later go straight through another intersection where there are tall pines ahead. The track becomes rough and rocky in places, crossing a dirt road beside a picnic

shelter around 1160m (3805ft) at **Morro Quemado**. The rugged track becomes a path, climbing past heather trees, cistus and broom. The path crosses a dirt road and climbs further, passing tall pines and broom. You'll walk over bare rock and later cross a pipeline in the forested **Barranco de Caramujo**. Cross a dirt road as signposted, followed by a higher crossing bearing marker posts, and then yet another dirt road, around 1400m (4595ft).

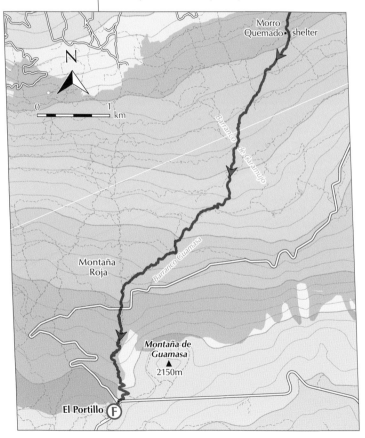

Join a track and followed it uphill. Eventually, marker posts indicate a path leaving the track, and the route switches between tracks and paths in quick succession, as indicated by more marker posts. There are rocky stretches on old lava flows among the pines, as well as a short stretch with crude stone paving. Keep an eye open to spot markers as the route switches between paths and tracks, as well as crossing a dirt road. By the time you reach **Montaña Roja**, around 1700m (5580ft), the slope is steep enough for the path to be zigzagging as it crosses a track.

Montaña de Guamasa is seen shortly before you reach El Portillo

While views have been dominated by pines for some time, there are now views into the steep-sided **Barranco Guamasa**. Cross a track and continue climbing towards a main road, passing beneath it through a tunnel, around 1810m (5940ft).

The path becomes more rugged underfoot, but also features a couple of stretches of old stone paving. The slopes alongside bear angular rocks and the pines become sparse in places. Eventually, the path leaves the pine forest and climbs a scrub-covered slope with views of nearby **Montaña de Guamasa** and the more distant El Teide. The path makes sweeping zigzags as it enters the Teide National Park, and eventually reaches a triangular junction where high-level roads meet at **El Portillo**, around 2040m (6700ft).

EL PORTILLO

The Restaurante El Portillo offers food and drink, with bus stops alongside. Unfortunately, there is no accommodation available anywhere nearby, and anyone caught wild camping can expect a severe telling-off. Trekkers with deep pockets can catch a bus through the Teide National Park and stay at the Parador hotel, with a view to returning by bus the following morning. Those looking for moderately priced accommodation should catch the bus down to La Orotava or Puerto de la Cruz for the night. Note that the two bus services can get very busy but, unlike all the other bus services on Tenerife, it is possible to book and pay online and reserve a seat at www. tomaticket.es/titsa-linea-348 or www.tomaticket.es/titsa-linea-342.

TEIDE NATIONAL PARK

The GR131 spends a day and a half in the Teide National Park, which is too little time to appreciate what this incredible place can offer. The highest mountain on Spanish territory, El Teide, raises its steep-sided volcanic cone to a summit of 3718m (12,198ft), flanked by the jagged mountainous rim of an awesome caldera. Naturally, some trekkers will wonder if they could climb it by diverting from the GR131 and, while this is possible, it needs a bit of advance planning. The national park is criss-crossed by signposted, waymarked and number-coded trails that would take in excess of a week to explore properly. If time can be spared, it is worth walking the short distance from El Portillo to the nearby National Park Visitor Centre, where a map of the park and its trails can be obtained, or tel 922 922 371.

Please note that access to almost all the trails through the national park, including the GR131, can be severely restricted at certain times when Corsican mouflon (wild sheep) are being hunted. If planning to walk here in May, June, October or November, please check in advance with the National Park Visitor Centre at El Portillo. The days when hunting takes place are usually Monday, Wednesday and Friday, but dates and times can vary, so always check in advance. Also, when snow and ice lie on El Teide, paths to and from the summit might be closed. If you can see snow on the mountain from a distance, and wish to make an ascent, please contact the national park visitor centre and check whether the paths are open or closed.

OPTIONAL ROUTE

Ascent of El Teide

Start	El Portillo
Finish	Parador
Distance	24.5km (15 miles)
Total ascent	1800m (5905ft)
Total descent	1590m (5215ft)
Time	2 days

For those who wish to include the summit of El Teide in their trek, the following notes explain how to link an ascent and descent into the course the GR131. Plan in advance in order to make a summit bid, as there are only two methods; either obtain a permit in advance or stay overnight at the Refugio Altavista and climb to the summit early the following morning. Access to the summit is strictly regulated and anyone turning up without observing the correct procedures will be turned away.

To obtain a permit in advance, go to www.reservasparquesnacionales. es and click on 'Teide'. Read and understand the regulations before applying for the permit. Be sure to carry a copy of the permit and your passport or government ID, as these have to be inspected before you are allowed to the summit.

To stay at the Refugio Altavista, go to www.volcanoteide.com and read about the regulations and available facilities before making a booking. Spending a night at the refuge allows you to climb to the summit of El Teide without a permit, so long as you leave the summit by 0900. Arrive any later and you will need a valid permit.

The following route description and statistics assume that you will start at El Portillo and climb to the Refugio Altavista during the day. The following day, it is assumed that you will climb to the summit of El Teide in time for the sunrise, then descend to the Parador to re-join the GR131. Trekkers who have proven reserves of energy and stamina might complete the traverse of the mountain in a single day, but bear in mind that it is often steep and rocky, as well as being high enough for some people to experience mild altitude sickness.

You could use the Teleférico del Teide cablecar service instead of walking. It is served by buses, but the cablecar doesn't link with the GR131, doesn't operate in high winds and can get exceptionally busy with long queues. For full details and online booking go to www.volcanoteide.com.

Day 1: El Portillo to Refugio Altavista
11.5km (7 miles), 1250m (4100ft) ascent, 20m (65ft) descent, 5hr

Leave El Portillo along the GR131, which follows a path running parallel to a main road. Turn right up a track and cross the main road to reach the national park **visitor centre**, where it is worth obtaining a free trail map. A series of numbered trails need to be linked together, so start by following the stone-paved S-1. This rises and falls, turns left through a gate to follow a fence, with a fine view of Montaña Blanca and El Teide ahead. The path rises and falls through three hollows full of scrub and light-coloured gravelly *jable*.

Turn left up the S-6 trail, climbing a path on crunchy *jable*. There is a view of El Teide at first, then shortly afterwards Montaña Blanca is seen again. The slopes are often bare and bright, sparsely dotted with broom and other scrub. There is no doubting the path, which always runs onwards and upwards at a gentle gradient, passing close to the cone of **Montaña de los Tomillos**.

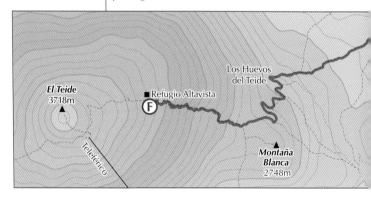

Later, the slope is bare and steep, and as the path climbs it passes a junction with the S-22 trail. However, keep climbing a little further to reach a track and a large sign at almost 2550m (8365ft).

The dusty white track is occasionally used by national park vehicles and is designated as the S-7 trail. Turn right and follow it, climbing round several bends. ▶ During the ascent, you pass many huge, round,

Don't short-cut, even if there are trodden paths, as national park staff get very annoyed.

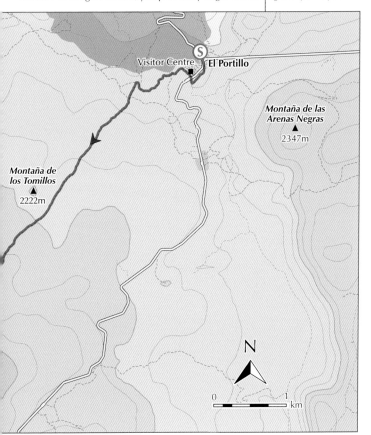

Sendero 6 is clear and obvious as it rises towards the foot of El Teide

These are Los Huevos del Teide, or 'Eggs of Teide'; lumps of lava that became detached from lava flows higher up the mountain, rolling down to where they now rest.

dark boulders. ◄ When a junction is reached, El Teide lies directly ahead. A short detour could be made to the left, onto the gentle **Montaña Blanca**, whose summit stands at 2748m (9016ft).

The path climbing the eastern flank of El Teide is steep and unrelenting, and it cannot be rushed. It is a dusty, gravelly path that zigzags tightly and endlessly, hemmed in on both sides by long, steep, dark tongues of lava. Looking up to the skyline, the summit cannot be seen, but you might notice a slender post that marks the position of the refuge. A few more 'Eggs of Teide' are passed and the path zigzags on a slope of gravel, boulders and broom. It then crosses a slope of reddish lava and is often on bare rock as it climbs further. There is little vegetation as the path gets close to the **Refugio Altavista**, around 3270m (10,730ft). The paved area in front of the building offers the chance to take a break on a level surface to enjoy the view.

The Refugio Altavista stands at 3270m (10,730ft) on El Teide

REFUGIO ALTAVISTA

It is always wise to make a reservation to stay at this refuge. Bear in mind that you must bring your own food and drink, noting that the water supply at the refuge is not drinkable. There are toilets and handbasins, but no shower. There is a basic kitchen, but no food is sold or served. The building generally opens at 1700 and it might not be until later that residents are allowed into the dormitory. Bear in mind that most residents plan to wake very early in the morning and will leave the refuge in the dark. Note that the building closes in the morning and belongings cannot be left behind.

Day 2: Refugio Altavista to Parador
13km (8 miles), 450m (1475ft) ascent, 1570m (5150ft) descent, 5hr
If you leave the Refugio Altavista very early in the morning, while it is still dark, be ready to use a head-torch. The path climbing beyond the refuge is gravelly underfoot and flanked by masses of blocky lava. An old ice cave lies to the right. The path becomes very uneven further uphill, being made of compacted boulders, but it is much easier to walk on than the huge angular blocks of lava to either side. The path climbs through a rocky defile and eventually reaches a junction with the S-11 trail.

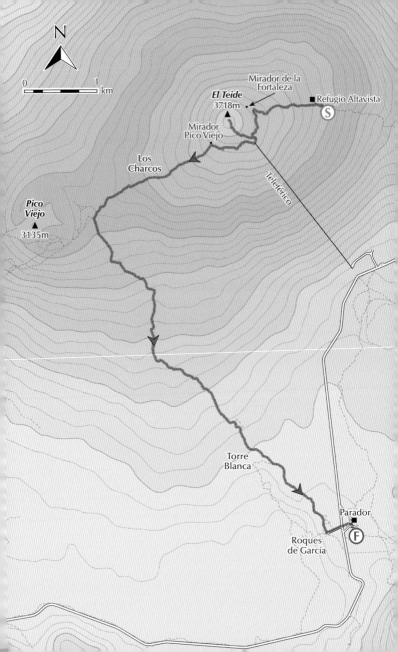

It is worth detouring to the right, where the path soon reaches the **Mirador de la Fortaleza**, around 3550m (11,645ft). ▸

If not making the detour, turn left along the path, which is known as La Rambleta. It wriggles across bouldery slopes, going up and down steps, reaching a junction with another path just before the *teleférico* station. This path is the Telesforo Bravo Trail, or S-10, and its use is strictly controlled. If you arrive from the refuge in time for sunrise, then no permit is required. If you arrive after 0900 then you need a permit, which must be arranged in advance. The path is obvious, stone-paved and zigzagging, climbing onto a cone that has only existed since 1798. Chains flank the path towards the top and fumaroles vent steam and sulphurous gases. There is no access to the crater, so stay on the path and scramble over blocks of rock to reach the summit of **El Teide** at 3718m (12,198ft), hopefully in time for sunrise. ▸

Remember that without a permit you must be off the summit before 0900, walking back down to the *teleférico* station, which should be running around this time. Walk past the station buildings to continue along the path, La Rambleta, now designated as the S-12 trail.

Fumaroles vent steam and sulphurous gases from the mountainside, and the rare *Gnaphalium teydeum* is one of the few plants that can survive such a hostile environment.

Usually, as the sun rises the conical peak throws a huge shadow across the 'sea of clouds' and it is often possible to spot five out of the seven Canary Islands.

Descending very rugged slopes from El Teide towards Pico Viejo

Casual visitors who arrive on the cablecar usually turn back at this point.

The last viewpoint is the **Mirador Pico Viejo**, at 3104m (10,184ft). ◄

A rugged path, the S-9 trail, descends steeply and cannot be hurried. Walk down past monstrous boulders at **Los Charcos**, then walk down beside a barranco-like gash in the lava, which the path later crosses. Continue down a steep and rugged black lava flow and pass some black boulders. The path continues much more easily down a gentle slope of soft, loose *jable*, where nothing grows. A broad gap is reached between El Teide and **Pico Viejo**, around 3080m (10,105ft). Unless tempted to detour onto Pico Viejo, turn left at a junction, down a path designated as S-23.

Continue the descent and the *jable* gives way to a winding, sandy path, later passing broom and gnarled rock, followed by a rugged path on lava. Pass a massive round boulder and make a short ascent, then walk down a winding, sandy path, later becoming rugged and dusty before dropping off the snout of a lava flow. The path continues descending, passing more distinctive, dark, round 'Eggs of Teide' on an easier stretch.

As the path continues its descent it steps up onto a lava flow, only to step down from it soon afterwards. There is a stretch across an old, crystalline lava flow that is difficult to trace, but the path becomes clearer afterwards. In fact, by the time the light-coloured pinnacles of **Torre Blanca** are reached, there is a junction with a much more obvious and popular path, the S-3 trail, around 2200m (7220ft). Turn left and follow this path past the amazing and intriguing Roque Cinchado and the rest of the towers and pinnacles of the **Roques de García**. When the path reaches a turning space, follow a road to a junction with the main road through the national park. Simply cross over and keep walking straight ahead to reach the **Parador**, its cafeteria and a national park visitor centre, around 2150m (6905ft). The GR131 is to the right, where there is a map-board and bus stop.

STAGE 22
El Portillo to Parador

Start	Restaurant, El Portillo
Finish	Bus stop, Parador
Distance	17km (10½ miles)
Total ascent	260m (855ft)
Total descent	150m (490ft)
Time	5hr
Terrain	Mostly easy walking along a gravel track with gentle gradients. A short, rugged path is used at the end.
Refreshments	Bar-restaurant at El Portillo. Cafeteria at the Parador.
Transport	TITSA bus 348 links Puerto de la Cruz with El Portillo and the Parador de las Cañadas del Teide. TITSA bus 342 links El Portillo with the Parador de las Cañadas del Teide, Vilaflor, Arona and Los Cristianos.
Accommodation	The Parador is the only option that does not involve a long bus ride off route.

This is one of the higher stages of the GR131, but also one of the easiest. If using bus services to arrive and leave, then be sure to monitor your pace throughout in order to catch your bus at the end of this stage. The only accommodation in the Teide National Park is at the expensive Parador hotel, reached by a 4km (2½ mile) spur from the main GR131 trail. Enjoy close-up views of El Teide throughout the day.

Start at **El Portillo**, around 2040m (6700ft), where there is a triangular road junction. Look for a roadside sign that states (wrongly) 'El Portillo 1980m'. A few steps drop from the road onto a narrow path, which is the GR131. The path drifts away from the road and later joins a track. ▶ Turn left to reach a junction, where a right turn is signposted for the Parador as S-4, also known as Siete Cañadas. Pass a barrier and the track is easy underfoot and obvious to follow for the rest of the day, rising gently to around 2100m (6890ft) near **Montaña de las Arenas Negras**.

Turn right if you wish to go to the nearby national park visitor centre.

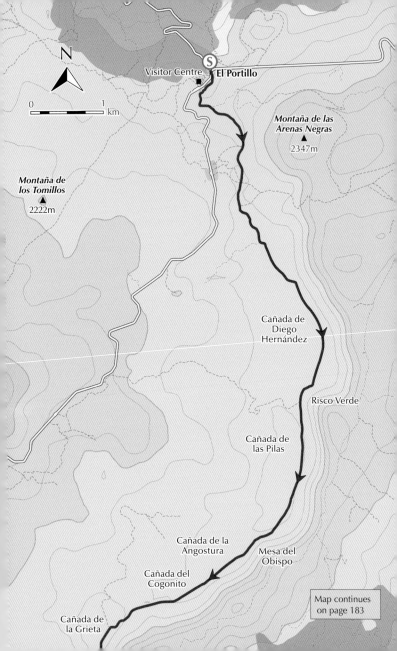

N

Visitor Centre · **El Portillo**
(S)

*Montaña de las
Arenas Negras*
▲
2347m

*Montaña de
los Tomillos*
▲
2222m

Cañada de
Diego
Hernández

Risco Verde

Cañada de
las Pilas

Cañada de la
Angostura

Mesa del
Obispo

Cañada del
Cogonito

Cañada de
la Grieta

Map continues
on page 183

0   1
km

The track has steep and jagged mountains rising to the left, which are part of the rim of an enormous caldera that encloses the national park. Light-coloured gravelly plains, or *cañadas*, often lie close to the track, with very rugged old lava flows beyond. These flows can be traced back to the enormous volcanic cone of El Teide. The first large gravelly plain is the **Cañada de Diego Hernández**. The route passes towers of red rock, as well as a signpost and lots of big boulders at the foot of **Risco Verde**.

The track crosses the **Cañada de las Pilas** and passes close to a cliff at the foot of the **Mesa del Obispo**. The plain of **Cañada de la Angostura** is narrow, being squeezed between mountains and lava flows. The track rises past the **Cañada del Cogonito** to reach the **Cañada de la Grieta**, at the foot of the shapely peak of **Topo de la Grieta**. ▶ Another stretch of the track is squeezed between the mountains and the snouts of old lava flows, before reaching the broad plain of **Cañada del Montón de Trigo**. Note a signpost pointing left for **Guajara**, which is on the S-5 trail, PR TF 86 and the GR131, but for the time being continue straight ahead, bearing in mind that you will return here the following day.

The dirt road passes easily around the foot of Guajara

Watch for tall tajinaste, or echiums, featuring masses of flowers when in bloom, turning to 'fish bones' when the plants die and dessicate.

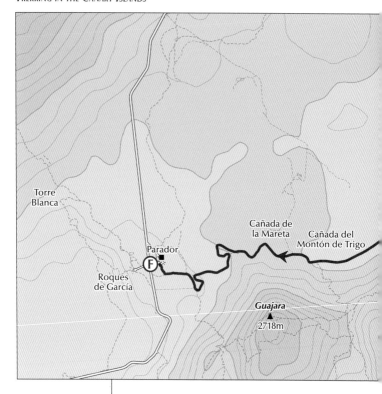

Pass a signposted junction and the track becomes very convoluted, passing close to amazing rock towers and buttresses, while climbing to around 2220m (7285ft), passing **Cañada de la Mareta**. Although a couple of bends might be short-cut, it is probably easier to stay on the track. The descent leads past a barrier and a little building called Caseta del Capricho. Turn right as signposted along a rather rough and stony path, passing scrub bushes. The path leads to a map-board beside a bus stop, with the buildings of the **Parador**, its cafeteria and a national park visitor centre nearby, around 2150m (6905ft).

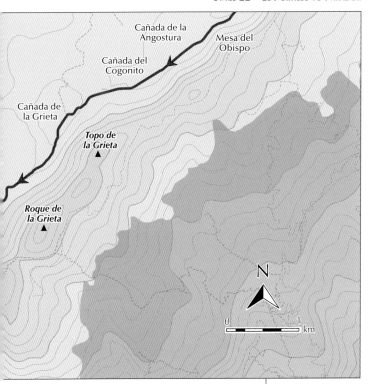

Cañada de la
Angostura

Mesa del
Obispo

Cañada del
Cogonito

Cañada de
la Grieta

*Topo de
la Grieta*
▲

*Roque de
la Grieta*
▲

N

0   1 km

PARADOR DE LAS CAÑADAS DEL TEIDE

The Parador offers the only accommodation in the national park, apart from the Refugio Altavista high on the slopes of El Teide. It is an expensive place to stay, but spending a night there would save a lot of travelling off-route by bus. (Discreet wild camping is difficult, though rock-climbers appear to make do with improvised bivouacs among nearby cliffs and boulders.) There is a cafeteria available, which tends to get very busy, as well as the nearby Ermita de las Nieves. The popular Roques de García lie within easy walking distance and are visited by cars and coachloads of tourists. The rock-forms are amazing, but the only way to avoid the crowds is to visit late in the evening or early in the morning.

STAGE 23
Parador to Vilaflor

Start	Bus stop, Parador
Finish	Church, Vilaflor
Distance	15.5km (9¾ miles)
Total ascent	380m (1245ft)
Total descent	1100m (3610ft)
Time	5hr 30min
Terrain	An easy start with a clear track. Rugged mountain paths are followed by easier forest paths and tracks. A very rugged old track is used on the final descent.
Refreshments	Cafeteria at the Parador. Plenty of choice at Vilaflor.
Transport	TITSA bus 342 links the Parador de las Cañadas del Teide, Vilaflor, Arona and Los Cristianos. TITSA bus 482 links Vilaflor with Arona and Los Cristianos. TITSA bus 474 links Vilaflor with Arona and Granadilla.
Accommodation	The Parador and a good choice in Vilaflor.

This stage sees the GR131 reach its highest point on its traverse through Tenerife. A rugged climb is necessary to leave the national park, then a rugged descent leads to easier forest paths and tracks. The village of Vilaflor offers all services, despite being around 1400m (4595ft) and prone to misty conditions. It is also an old settlement that is worth exploring.

A bus stop and map-board stand in a turning area near the **Parador**, around 2150m (7055ft). Follow a rather rough and stony path gently downhill past scrub bushes. Turn left as signposted along a clear and obvious track, retracing steps of the previous day, passing a little building called Caseta del Capricho and a barrier. There are awesome rock outcrops, buttresses and towers in view and the track is quite convoluted as it climbs, levelling out around 2220m (7285ft), passing **Cañada de la Mareta**. Descend to cross a small gravelly plain then rise gently to pass a signposted junction with another track and keep straight ahead.

Climbing towards the Degollada de Guajara with El Teide beyond

Look back to El Teide, which will later be lost to view.

Turn right as signposted up a path marked as the S-5 trail, PR TF 86 and the GR131. Views open up across the vast caldera, with the massive volcanic cone of El Teide always in view. The path winds uphill and eventually reaches an abundance of signposts and noticeboards on the rocky gap of **Degollada de Guajara**, at almost 2390m (7840ft). ◄ Turn right to follow a rugged path across the slopes of **Guajara**, but don't be drawn to the right unless you intend to make a bid for the summit. The path rises onto a shoulder and passes a noticeboard. The highest point on the GR131 through Tenerife lies somewhere around 2420m (7940ft) on a virtually level path.

The path becomes rather rough and rocky as its starts descending, though considerable effort has been made in the past to move boulders to either side to facilitate passage. The route passes a stand of pine trees; other pines are rather sparse on the rocky mountainside. Within the space of a single stride, the rock gives way to a barren slope of crunchy black ash. The path is flanked by lines of stones brought down from the mountain, supplemented with broken chunks of concrete. The descent is a dead straight line, but be ready to make a sudden turn to the right when indicated by marker posts.

The path is flanked by short wooden posts for a while, then there are rocks poking through the ash on the way across the **Barranco de las Arenas**, around 2070m (6790ft). The path rises a little, then descends through sparse pine forest, crossing a rocky patch. Shortly afterwards, look down to the right to spot an outcrop of light-coloured rock cut into fluted forms – the **Paisaje Lunar** (Lunar Landscape). Continue down through the forest to reach a junction with another signposted path and turn right. Shortly afterwards, pass an old water channel. The track is plain and obvious, but sometimes it is quite rough and stony underfoot. The pines are fairly short and widely spaced, so there are frequent views of the surrounding area. Cross the bed of the **Barranco Eris de Carnero** and later drop through a cutting in bright, lightweight, gravelly *jable*.

The track continues its gentle descent, passing a ruin before reaching a barrier at a junction with a dirt road. Simply cross over the road and go down a narrow and obvious path. At one point you'll come across a big pine tree that has stone seats beneath it. A further descent leads to another signposted junction. Turn right and go down stone steps to reach another dirt road, where there are more signposts. Turn right and almost immediately turn left to find another path running down through the forest. There is some very uneven stone paving as the path zigzags down across the bed of the **Barranco de las Mesas**, around 1600m (5250ft).

Climb steeply for a short way and go through a gap in a low drystone wall. On the other side of the wall, widely spaced walls flank a track that follows a water pipe down past stoutly walled cultivation terraces at **Casa Galinda**. There are marker posts and a signpost, but the descent is obvious. The old track has lost much of its original surface, leaving so much uneven bedrock exposed that it is rougher than most mountain trails on the GR131. It is certainly no longer capable of accommodating wheeled vehicles. The track narrows to a path, just before reaching a junction with another track around 1390m (4560ft).

Turn left down the track, then turn right up a rugged, stone-paved path. At its highest point the path is broad

Crumbling jable is passed on the forested descent to Vilaflor

and features much more recent stone paving, as well as a plaque commemorating its restoration. Turn left down a road, then keep right at a couple more road junctions and walk up into the village of **Vilaflor**. Tarmac gives way to a stone-paved road in the Centro Histórico. Walk up through a well-planted square to reach the church and keep to the left-hand side of the building to find a GR131 signpost around 1430m (4690ft).

VILAFLOR

Dating from the 16th century, Vilaflor de Chasna is located high on pine-clad mountainsides, with enough water to support agriculture and a water-bottling plant. Old mills can be seen tucked into a valley beside the village and old houses abound. There is a range of accommodation, bar-restaurants, shops, crafts, ATM and bus services.

STAGE 24
Vilaflor to Arona

Start	Church, Vilaflor
Finish	Bus stop, Arona
Distance	8km (11 miles)
Total ascent	450m (1475ft)
Total descent	1260m (4135ft)
Time	6hr
Terrain	Roads and tracks give way to convoluted forest paths that are steep and rugged in places. Roads, tracks and paths are linked on the final descent to Arona.
Refreshments	Plenty of choice at Vilaflor. Bar-restaurant at Ifonche. Also plenty of choice at Arona.
Transport	TITSA bus 482 links Vilaflor with Arona and Los Cristianos. TITSA bus 474 links Arona with Granadilla, whereas TITSA bus 416 runs to Los Cristianos.
Accommodation	Available in Vilaflor and Arona, plus plenty of choice in Los Cristianos.

The final stage of the GR131 through Tenerife generally runs downhill, but still includes several uphill stretches. After wandering through pine forests the route descends to Ifonche, then passes the remarkable peak of Roque Imoque. You'll pass steep and rugged slopes bearing old cultivation terraces on the way down to the little town of Arona, where buses connect with Los Cristianos and its ferry-port.

Face the church in **Vilaflor** and look around the left-hand side to spot a GR131 signpost. Follow the road indicated, Calle Los Molinos, which bends and rises to a main road. Cross over and go straight up a steep road as signposted. Watch out on the right to spot a flight of stone steps and go up them. A paved path runs high above the road, passing a chapel before re-joining the road. Follow the road to its end, where it passes between the splendid **Hotel VillAlba** and a football ground.

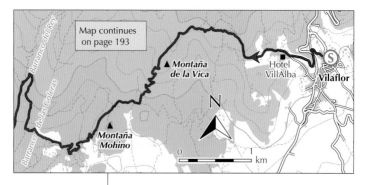

A broad and rugged track is signposted, running into a pine forest. A clearing contains cultivation terraces covered in bright, gravelly *jable*. Stay on the main track, which is rather rocky, rising back into pine forest. Turn right at a junction to climb to a white-painted concrete reservoir on the forested slope. Keep left to pass it and the rocky track has a water pipe alongside. Follow this up to a signposted junction and turn left along a path, still following the water pipe. Eventually, cross a rocky little gap around 1615m (5300ft). ◀

Look out across the sea, or 'sea of clouds' to spot La Gomera and El Hierro.

Go down stone steps, where cistus flourishes on the rocky ground, and the pines have obviously seen forest fires in the past. The path passes near a cliff edge, then, further downhill, rocky ground gives way to a crunchy red path. Follow this faithfully, avoiding other paths that have been worn by motor-bikers on the slopes of **Montaña de la Vica**. The path often has a slight stone-built edge and most of the zigzag bends feature a few log steps. Reach a tangle of water pipes and follow them down to a track. Turn right and go through a track intersection as signposted. Climb past terraces and follow the forest track to a turning area, around 1370m (4495ft).

A path is signposted, rising gently across the slopes of **Montaña Mohino**. When it descends, keep to the right where a water pipe crosses. A rocky path drops past old terraces, then occasional log steps continue down the forested slope. A path is marked as it crosses an old track twice while descending. After swinging right, the path drops into the **Barranco de las Goleras** and crosses a stone-arched bridge, around 1240m (4070ft).

Climb from the bridge, passing a cultivation terrace and cross an old broken water channel. The path rises to a small reservoir, then goes down a flight of log steps and passes old terraces. Climb, and as there is another deep barranco ahead, swing right and follow a vague path straight up a rocky, forested slope. Eventually, pass a warning notice and cross the bed of the **Barranco del Rey**, around 1380m (4530ft). Walk up a stone-paved path, then follow a rugged path downhill, soon passing a circular *era*, or old threshing floor. Continue down the slope and a few stone and log steps later drop more steeply on **Ladera Grande**. The path zigzags, then there is a rough and rocky ridge ahead, where a fence runs alongside part of the path.

Continue downhill, zigzagging again and crossing the bed of another barranco. Climb from the pine forest, passing cistus and prickly pears to reach a signpost beside a dirt road. Turn left and follow the dirt road to join a tarmac road, later reaching a staggered crossroads at **Ifonche**, passing the Bar Restaurante El Dornajo, around 1020m (3345ft).

A path through forest near the Barranco del Rey

An era, *or threshing floor, below the peak of Roque Imoque*

Follow the road onwards, keeping right at a fork, passing an abrupt edge where paragliders sometimes launch themselves into a deep valley. Go straight past a junction where there is a wooden cross and eventually reach the end of the road beside a house. Turn right as signposted down a path, reaching a gap and another circular *era*, at 987m (3238ft), beneath the towering peak of **Roque Imoque**.

Keep right and follow a fenced path as it cuts across a steep slope, descending by exploiting a soft ochre layer sandwiched between harder rock. ◀ Pass a water channel and note how it is later cut into the rock. Continue down to a gap at 827m (2680ft), where there is yet another circular *era* and a water channel. Keep to the right, rising and falling, passing daisies, prickly pears, *cardón* and a rocky gap at 759m (2490ft).

Turn left and walk down through a valley, passing another *era* and a ruin. Warning signs flank a rocky barranco, alerting trekkers to the dangers of flash flooding. Climb and pass another sign warning of rock-fall from an

There is a view of Arona, but the way to the village is convoluted.

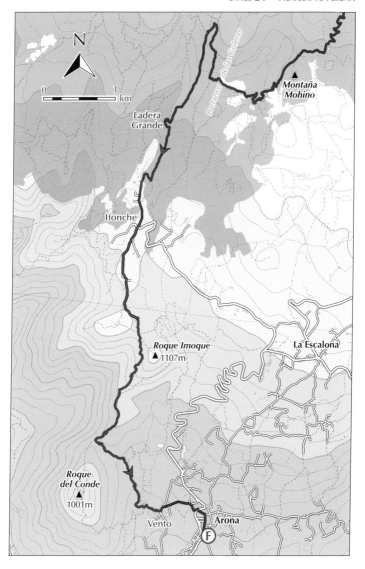

overhang. Follow a path beside a tall fence until you reach a signposted junction. Turn left and the path leads across a couple of streambeds before rising and following a road past houses. Turn left at a junction, along Calle Vento in the little village of **Vento**. Turn right at a roundabout to continue along Calle Mazape. Follow this road straight ahead and later use a pedestrian crossing on a main road.

Walk straight into **Arona** as indicated, reaching the church of San Antonio Abad on the Plaza Cristo de la Salud. The final GR131 map-board and signpost are located behind the church. To finish properly, go straight down Calle Domínguez Alfonso and turn left at the bottom, to find Arona's bus stop on the Plaza La Paz, which was formerly a cemetery, around 600m (1970ft).

ARONA

This little town offers accommodation, bar-restaurants, shops and a range of other services, but most trekkers will probably want to catch a bus down to Los Cristianos to catch a ferry to La Gomera and the next stretch of the GR131.

TENERIFE TO LA GOMERA

The trek through Tenerife concludes in Arona, where TITSA bus 482 can be used to get straight down to the brash and busy resort of Los Cristianos. If a night has to be spent here, then there is abundant accommodation and every kind of service, but be sure to check the ferry sailings for La Gomera and, if necessary, be ready to make an early start in the morning.

Two ferry companies sail regularly between Los Cristianos on Tenerife and San Sebastián on La Gomera. Fred Olsen ferries take 50min to sail between the islands, and Naviera Armas take 1hr for the crossing. If there is a chance of getting an evening sailing to San Sebastián and accommodation in the town centre, then the trek along the GR131 can re-commence early the following morning.

It is worth enquiring about ferries to La Palma and El Hierro before leaving Los Cristianos. An efficient completion of the trek along the GR131 hinges on getting good ferry connections, or you risk losing entire days because of poor connections.

Fred Olsen, tel 902 100 107 www.fredolsen.es

Naviera Armas, tel 902 456 500 www.navieraarmas.com

LA GOMERA

Mist gathers around the prominent Roque de Agando (Stage 25)

LA GOMERA
45.5km (28¹/₄ miles) 2 days

The GR131 runs coast to coast across the little island of La Gomera and can be completed in as little as two days. However, the long first stage presented in this guidebook might be a little too much for some trekkers; it can be cut short by catching a bus at one of several points on the higher parts of the route.

Given the small size of the island, some might wonder if the entire route could be covered from a single base. Although this is possible, a study of the bus timetables reveals that the main town of San Sebastián isn't ideally placed for this approach, since the buses into the mountains don't leave town until quite late in the morning. In fact, the best base is surprisingly the mountain village of Chipude, where many of the island's bus services pass from early until late each day.

The GR131 across La Gomera starts with a steady climb from San Sebastián towards the high, forested parts of the island. The forest is a remnant of the laurisilva forest that once dominated the tropics, and the one on La Gomera is reckoned to be one of the best surviving examples in the world, although it suffered recent fire damage. The highest point on the island is passed at Garajonay, at 1484m (4869ft). After visiting a series of high villages and passing through the laurisilva forest again, the route descends to Vallehermoso and completes its coast-to-coast crossing on the island.

TRANSPORT

GuaguaGomera bus services operate out of San Sebastián and basically run parallel to the GR131 all the way through upland villages of Chipude, El Cercado and Las Hayas. Bus services are available at Vallehermoso for the return journey to San Sebastián. Check the website for full details of services, www.guaguagomera.com or tel 922 141 101.

TOURIST INFORMATION

The main tourism website for La Gomera is www.lagomera.travel. Although there are a few tourist information offices around the island, only one of them is useful for visiting trekkers:

•   San Sebastián, tel 922 141 512

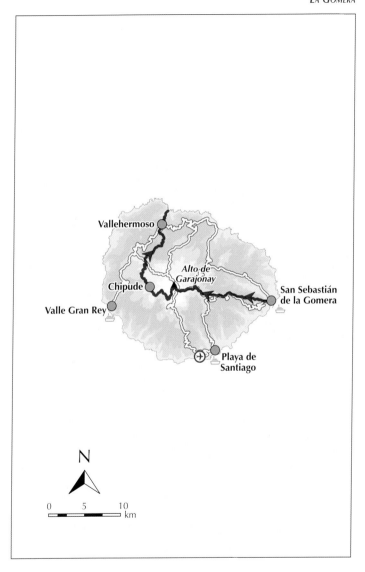

STAGE 25
San Sebastián to Chipude

Start	Ferry-port, San Sebastián
Finish	Hotel Sonia, Chipude
Distance	27km (16¾ miles)
Total ascent	1960m (6430ft)
Total descent	880m (2885ft)
Time	10hr
Terrain	Roads, tracks and rugged paths alternate, climbing from scrub-covered slopes to forested slopes, later passing from village to village.
Refreshments	Plenty of choice at San Sebastián. Bar-restaurant at Degollada de Peraza. Bar-restaurant at Los Apartaderos. Bar-restaurant at Chipude.
Transport	GuaguaGomera bus 1 links San Sebastián, Degollada de Peraza, Roque de Agando, Pajarito, Igualero and Chipude with Las Hayas and Valle Gran Rey. GuaguaGomera bus 3 links San Sebastián with Degollada de Peraza, Playa de Santiago and the airport. GuaguaGomera bus 6 links the airport with Igualero, Chipude and Valle Gran Rey.
Accommodation	Plenty of choice in San Sebastián and a hotel in Chipude.

The GR131 climbs steadily from sea level at San Sebastián to the highest point on La Gomera, on the summit of Garajonay. The ascent passes steep slopes of scrub and old terraces, as well as occasional farms to reach higher forest. After passing the awesome Roque de Agando the route follows a forested crest towards Garajonay. Mountain paths and tracks link Igualero with Pavón to reach Chipude.

Although the GR131 starts in the centre of **San Sebastián**, it is worth walking from the ferry-port into town to locate the first signpost. Follow a long blue line painted on the ground, running from the ferry-port along a broad pavement beside a marina. At the point where the line ends, you'll see the first signpost straight ahead, and a marker post lies just beyond it. Turn right at the marker post and use a pedestrian crossing to reach the Plaza de las Américas. Turn left to reach an adjacent park surrounded by stout iron fencing, and notice another marker post. ▶

Follow the fence around the park, first on its seaward side, then turn right along the Avenida del V Centenario. You'll reach a roundabout near the bus station and, while a map-board and signpost look promising, these are actually for the long-distance GR132, which encircles La Gomera. Cross a bridge over a wide and usually dry riverbed to find a combined GR131 and GR132 signpost. There is a small roundabout, and the road to follow is the Cañada del Herrero. This climbs past a sports ground, where a 'Km1' marker stands. ▶

At the top of the road you'll reach another roundabout. Turn left along the short Calle Isla de Lobos, then turn right to follow Avenida de las Galanas to the last house in **Las Galanas**. Turn left along a short tarmac road where there is a map-board and signpost, around 100m (330ft). Turn right as marked up a path, which is plain and obvious as it climbs a rugged slope of rock, *tabaibal*, *verode* and *aulaga*. The path, featuring broken rock and boulder paving, climbs past Km2 and Km3 markers, with fine views back to San Sebastián, Tenerife and El Teide.

The white-painted Torre del Conde dates from the 15th century. Christopher Columbus visited it on his way to the Americas.

Note that all the streets heading to the left are named after different Canary Islands.

High above San Sebastián, looking across the sea to Tenerife

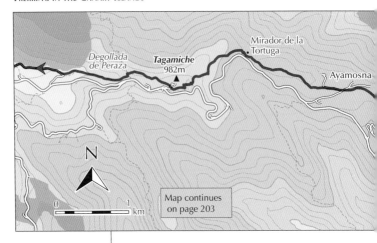

Degollada de Peraza

Tagamiche 982m ▲

Mirador de la • Tortuga

Ayamosna

N ▲

0 ———— 1 km

Map continues on page 203

The path reaches a road near a few houses at **El Pajar del Higueral**, around 410m (1345ft). Turn left for a short road-walk, then turn right up another rugged path. This runs parallel to the road then pulls away from it, joining it again on a bend. Follow the road uphill but use a short path on the right as marked, quickly re-joining the road near a palm tree and a small stone building. Further up the road, a path can be used to short-cut a bend but, rather oddly, the route follows the road, so it is your choice.

Another longer stretch of path avoids the road then later crosses it. Follow the path higher and a newly stone-paved stretch passes to the right of a fenced compound. The paving ends on a crest at the Km5 marker, around 670m (2200ft). A track continues, passing boulder-strewn slopes where there is a huddle of farm buildings above at **Ayamosna**. When you reach a map-board near a road junction, follow the road up towards another farm. A rugged path keeps to the left of the farm and its access road, passing a few palm trees and the Km6 marker.

Palms and agaves sprout at intervals from slopes of rugged scrub. The **Mirador de la Tortuga** is passed on a gap at 773m (2356ft). The path climbs and passes some palms and a lonesome pine.

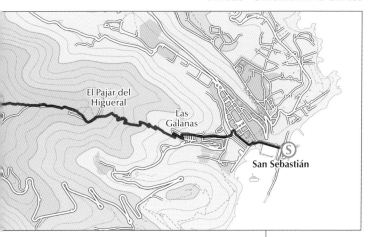

A summit ahead, **Tagamiche**, is crowned by a mast and the path zigzags uphill, passing to the left of it. A descent leads to a track, where a right turn leads across a concrete track and past a white building. A signpost points down a path, where stone steps drop to pass a pylon. Cross a steep slope of cistus and pass the Km9 marker. Water collects behind a wall before a fenced stretch of the path rises and falls as it traverses a cliff. ▶ Fig trees and palm trees grow at a path junction. Turn left as signposted and zigzag up to a road, bus shelter and viewpoint at **Degollada de Peraza**, at 946m (3104ft). Turn left to get to a bar-restaurant, otherwise turn right to continue.

There are a few trees, which will become more common once the laurisilva forest is reached later, and of course beware of rock-fall.

There is no need to step onto the road. Stone steps go up and down to pass a tower of rock, then the path runs behind a roadside barrier where there is a rock-fall warning. Climb 49 stone steps and follow a bouldery path past heather trees. A track rises along a more open crest, passing the Km10 marker. Keep right at a junction to pass close to a house. Walk between more heather trees then turn right up a road. Towards the top of the road, turn right up a rugged paved path, quickly reaching the **Ermita de las Nieves**, around 1120m (3675ft). The

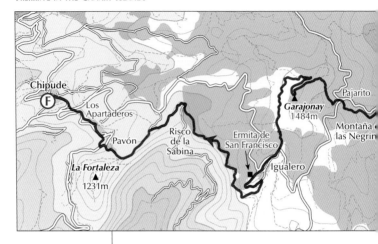

chapel and picnic area are surrounded by tall pines, but in most other directions there are heather trees.

There is a map-board and a signpost pointing the way ahead. Follow a track, then later go down a deeply sunken path among more heather trees. Continue down log steps and a rocky slope to reach a road. Stay behind the roadside barrier round a broad bend beneath the enormous **Roque de Agando**, then, after passing the Km13 marker, cross the road to reach a rusty monument and climb 65 stone steps. Reach the road again after avoiding a bend and turn left to find a bus shelter and a fine viewpoint looking back to the Roque de Agando.

Cross the road to follow a path that falls and rises, zigzagging up and down log steps before crossing the road again at a higher level. As the path climbs through dense laurisilva forest, two left turns could be used to reach a hilltop viewpoint, otherwise keep straight ahead at both junctions, bearing in mind that there are occasional good views anyway. A footbridge crosses a road bend, then a path runs along a wooded, flowery crest around 1300m (4265ft). Cross over the road and climb stone steps, following a paved path to reach the **Mirador de Tajaqué**. ◄

There might be a view of the distant island of La Palma.

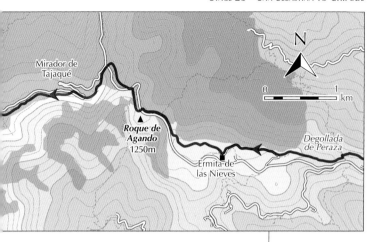

The path runs behind a roadside barrier and passes the Km15 marker. Drop from the road, wandering through a fire-damaged part of the laurisilva forest. Climb zigzag log steps, then the track almost reaches the road, but a path leaves and climbs along the high crest. There are long flights of log steps as the path negotiates the roller-coaster crest of **Montaña de las Negrinas**. When the path reaches a track, turn right and follow it down to a roundabout and bus shelter at **Pajarito**, over 1350m (4430ft).

A track on the other side of the roundabout is signposted for Alto de Garajonay. Follow it, but quickly turn right to climb a long flight of log steps. This is another roller-coaster stretch, with every short descent followed by a longer climb on log steps, and a signpost indicating a left turn at a junction. Cross a final gap and climb to the summit of **Garajonay**, at 1484m (4869ft). A wall surrounds the summit and there are views in all directions across the forested uplands of the national park.

Notices explain how the summit of **Garajonay** was used by ancient Gomeros for ritual purposes. The summit was excavated by archaeologists, who then buried the site and recreated a replica on top of it. In clear weather it is possible to look back to El Teide on Tenerife, as well as looking ahead to La Palma and El Hierro.

Leave the summit by walking down a stone-paved access road, later turning left as signposted along a dirt road. Keep left again at another junction, passing the Km19 marker. Keep left at yet another track junction, then turn right as signposted down stone steps. Some of these are quite rugged and there are almost 150 of them leading down to a bus shelter on a road bend, around 1330m (4365ft). Turn right along the road, then left down another road, then right up a path. The path rises parallel to the road and later joins it again at a junction.

Turn left as signposted and follow the road past a viewpoint car park beside the little **Ermita de San Francisco**. The road bends left as it descends and later keeps straight ahead at a junction, entering the tiny village of **Igualero**. Watch for a path dropping to the right, which is roughly stone-paved, passing the Km21 marker. Although the path is rugged, it is also obvious, and it is only necessary to keep right at a signposted junction. There are often pines above the path, while areas of former laurisilva forest were burnt in 2012. The path passes two pylons and roughly contours around 1200m (3935ft). After passing above the cliffs and rugged slopes of **Risco de la Sabina**, the path descends past the Km23 marker and drops to a road bend in the Barranco del Nogal, around 1120m (3675ft).

Turn right and follow the road up to another prominent bend then turn left as signposted down a path. This is plain and obvious, eventually reaching a junction. ◄ Turn right and walk down a stone-paved path, followed by a new stone-paved road in the little village of **Pavón**. Keep left down a tarmac road, then a rough stone-paved road leads down to another road. Turn left and keep behind the roadside barrier, then turn sharp right down into the Barranco de Iguala. A short, steep climb leads back to the road, where a left turn leads past the Bar Los Camioneros in the little village of Los Apartaderos.

Turn left for a steep and rocky scramble to the summit of La Fortaleza.

Turn right up another road, then later, once it starts to drop, turn right up a concrete track to reach a house. Drop to a rugged path to reach the road and turn right. Watch on the right for another concrete road, which climbs to a road and a bus shelter. Cross the road and walk down a concrete and rough stone-paved road, turning right at the bottom to follow a road into the village of **Chipude**, around 1080m (3545ft). Accommodation is available at the Hotel Sonia and there is also a shop and an ATM. Buses pass through the village in both directions from early until late.

The rocky prominence of La Fortaleza, above Pavón

STAGE 26
Chipude to Playa de Vallehermoso

Start	Hotel Sonia, Chipude
Finish	Playa de Vallehermoso
Distance	18.5km (11½ miles)
Total ascent	420m (1380ft)
Total descent	1500m (4920ft)
Time	6hr
Terrain	Cultivated terraces give way to laurisilva forest, followed by a long descent, steep at times, into a valley. A rugged ascent and descent are followed by an easy valley walk to the coast.
Refreshments	Bar-restaurants at Chipude, El Cercado and Las Hayas. Plenty of choice at Vallehermoso.
Transport	GuaguaGomera bus 1 links Chipude, El Cercado and Las Hayas with San Sebastián and Valle Gran Rey. GuaguaGomera bus 6 links Chipude, El Cercado and Las Hayas with Valle Gran Rey and the airport. GuaguaGomera bus 2 links Vallehermoso with San Sebastián.
Accommodation	Hotel in Chipude, plenty of choice in Vallehermoso.

The GR131 starts at a relatively high level and wanders from village to village before heading straight through laurisilva 'cloud forest'. When mist brushes the trees, drips fall to the ground as if it was raining, keeping the island well supplied with water. A long descent with a bit of a sting in its tail leads to the village of Vallehermoso, then a simple valley walk takes you to the end of the trail on the northern coast.

Walk across the road from the Hotel Sonia in **Chipude** to find map-boards, with a stone-paved road signposted behind them. This road quickly gives way to a concrete path, which in turn gives way to a more rugged path that drops to a road. Turn right along the road until another path is signposted down into the green **Barranco de los Manantiales**. Make your way over a streambed and

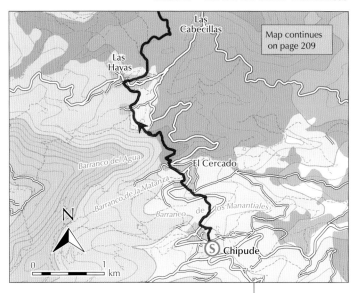

climb, crossing a road, until you reach a crest. Go down a concrete track that quickly gives way to a path down to a road. Cross over the road and follow a stone-paved path down to another road. Turn right to follow this road round the **Barranco de la Matanza**, then turn left as marked along a concrete path, until steps lead up to a road at the Bar Victoria in the village of **El Cercado**, around 1040m (3410ft).

Turn left and quickly reach the Bar María, where a stone-paved path descends from a map-board and signpost. The path becomes more rugged, but remains clear, crossing a streambed in the **Barranco del Agua**, passing the Km28 marker. Follow a terrace path and later cross another streambed, then climb some crude stone steps. ▸ The path climbs, levels out and goes straight ahead at a junction. Go down log steps and walk along a terrace flanked by palm trees, passing the Km29 marker. Pass another junction and go up a short, steep road and over a crossroads before walking down Calle

Warning notices flank a rocky overhang.

207

Los Eucaliptos. Palm trees grow alongside, but there are big eucalyptus trees at a crossroads, where there is also a map-board, signpost and the Restaurante Efigenia at **Las Hayas**, around 1010m (3315ft).

Turn right and walk up to a junction where there is a national park signpost and go up a narrow road that soon gives way to a path. Follow a track past a chapel and continue up a path into laurisilva forest. Pass a notice marking the limit of the Garajonay National Park, as well as the Km30 marker. The path passes leaning, contorted heather trees and reaches a signposted junction with a track at **Las Cabecillas**. Turn right and follow the gently undulating track, later reaching a clearing where there is a picnic site and a signposted junction. Turn left along a track (not a path) and pass the Km32 marker. The track rises to a road where there are signposts and a bus shelter, around 1070m (3510ft).

Turn left and follow a path behind a roadside barrier. This later turns away from the road and once the descent commences on the slopes of **Montaña de la Araña** it becomes quite steep. Turn right at a path junction at Risquillo de Corgo, then go down flights of log steps. There is a gentler stretch along a high crest, passing a notice,

Old paths are followed between Chipude and El Cercado

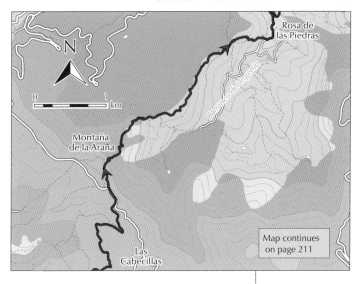

Map continues on page 211

then the path steepens and there are more flights of log steps past the Km34 marker. The path crosses a track at 745m (2445ft), where the forest begins to feature a wider selection of plants, including abundant prickly pears.

The path mostly keeps to the right of the high crest but occasionally runs along the top of it. Yet more flights of log steps continue the descent and a fine rocky peak is passed. Eventually, the path reaches a junction where the GR131 used to turn left, but now it turns right. Log steps and stone steps zigzag downhill, passing vines at one point. At length the path comes to a road deep in the **Barranco del Ingenio**. Turn left and walk down the road to **Rosa de las Piedras**, where marker posts indicate a right turn to reach a picnic site and map-boards, around 330m (1080ft).

Turn right again to follow a rather battered road around the far side of the reservoir of **Presa de la Encantadora**. Beside the dam you'll reach concrete steps where a path on the right soon passes the Km38 marker. A steep climb with a few log steps proves a little arduous. Cross a crest around 420m (1380ft) and follow a path

A wet day in the laurisilva 'cloud forest' above Las Hayas

onwards, generally losing height while admiring a huge tower of rock ahead. The path becomes quite rocky but eventually gives way to a concrete path passing houses at **La Fortaleza**. A bendy road completes the descent, then climbs a little to reach a road junction. Turn right, then turn left at another junction beside the Bar-Restaurante Triana and follow the road into a fine plaza in the middle of **Vallehermoso**, around 170m (560ft).

VALLEHERMOSO

This busy little town is located where several deep, steep-sided barrancos meet, flanked by steep and rocky mountains. A good range of services are available and it is quite likely that the town will be visited twice, as most people will finish the GR131 shortly after passing through, then return to make onward progress. There is a range of accommodation, plenty of bar-restaurants and shops, bus services and taxis. Talk to a taxi driver before leaving, if you want to be picked up at the end of the trail.

Just beyond the plaza lies a roundabout where there is a signpost, with a map-board just beyond. Follow the road signposted for Playa de Vallehermoso, walking down past a little bus station, then turn right at a road junction. As soon as the road bends left, turn right down a path, then turn left down a streambed and left again down a riverbed in the **Barranco del Valle**. Cross a footbridge and climb

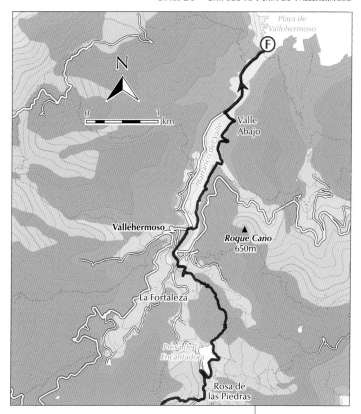

a little, then follow a terrace path overlooking the fertile floor of the barranco. ▶ At one point a chain is fixed to a stout wall where the path is rather narrow.

On reaching a signposted junction with another path, keep left to continue. The terrace quickly comes to a road near a house. Follow the road until it crosses the valley at **Valle Abajo** to reach a junction and a bus shelter. Turn right to walk down the road, all the way to its end at the **Playa de Vallehermoso**, where there are mapboards and signposts.

Look across to a botanical garden which has suffered years of neglect.

The prominent Roque Cano is seen on the descent to Vallehermoso

The GR131 finishes at **Playa de Vallehermoso**, but is joined by the GR132, which makes a circuit all the way around La Gomera. There is a failed café and pool at the road-end, along with an abandoned restaurant at Castillo del Mar, where bananas were once loaded onto boats using a crane. The black pebble beach is hemmed in by cliffs, and all that can be seen out to sea is part of the Teno peninsula on neighbouring Tenerife.

LA GOMERA TO LA PALMA

Getting an efficient transfer between the end of the GR131 on La Gomera and the continuation of the trail on La Palma requires careful planning in order to avoid delays. The easiest way to leave Playa de Vallehermoso is to take a taxi back to Vallehermoso. From there GuaguaGomera bus 2 runs to San Sebastián, where the ferry-port is within easy walking distance of the bus station.

Two ferry companies sail between San Sebastián on La Gomera and Santa Cruz on La Palma. Naviera Armas ferries generally sail mid-afternoon and take 2hr 15min to reach La Palma. That sailing could be too early for trekkers. Fred Olsen ferries generally sail in the evening and take 2hr to reach La Palma. However, if using the late ferry it is wise to have accommodation pre-booked, close to the harbour in Santa Cruz, and inform your hosts that you will be arriving late.

Fred Olsen, tel 902 100 107 www.fredolsen.es

Naviera Armas, tel 902 456 500 www.navieraarmas.com

LA PALMA

A clear path climbs slopes of loose black ash (Stage 27)

LA PALMA
69.5km (43¼ miles) 4 days

The first stretch of the GR131 to be established was on La Palma, in 1999. The trail across the island is quite tough and stays as high as possible. The route is described from south to north, starting from Faro de Fuencaliente in the extreme south of the island, as this is the most gradual way to handle the arduous climb from sea level to the highest mountain. Well-worn paths climb slopes of crunchy black volcanic ash to reach Fuencaliente. The route passes several volcanoes on the Cumbre Vieja, including a number that have erupted since the Conquest and were recorded by historians.

The Cumbre Nueva is largely forested, though sparsely so in places, and the trees eventually give way to rocky mountains covered in scrub bushes. The awesome gulf of the Caldera de Taburiente, protected as a national park, is seen from all angles, though there are no safe ways to descend into it. After reaching the highest point on the island, at the Roque de los Muchachos, the GR131 passes a few other summits, then begins a steep and steady descent to the coast at Puerto de Tazacorte.

As much of the GR131 runs high and is remote from settlements, it is best suited to those who carry full

Rugged lava on Volcán Teneguía with Volcán de San Antonio above (Stage 27)

backpacking kit and pay particular attention to keeping themselves hydrated. Operating from a base such as Santa Cruz is possible, and buses can certainly be used at the start and finish, but accessing other points on the trail would require the use of taxis, and several trips would become quite expensive.

There are no direct ferries or flights for onward travel from La Palma to the final island of El Hierro. To enable a smooth transfer, the connections back through La Gomera or Tenerife will need careful planning.

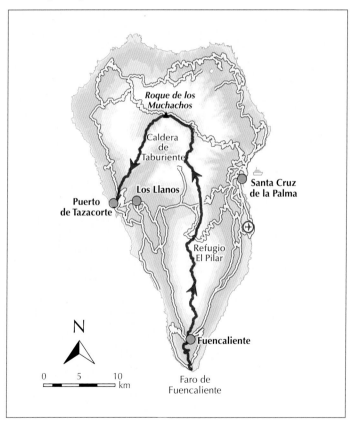

215

The descent from Volcán de la Deseada towards Refugio El Pilar (Stage 28)

TRANSPORT

Transportes Insular La Palma (TILP) buses offer a good level of service around and across La Palma, but only rarely connect with the GR131. Getting from Santa Cruz to Fuencaliente is easy and there are connecting buses down to Faro de Fuencaliente, where the GR131 starts. However, buses crossing La Palma go through a tunnel beneath the Cumbre Nueva, so they don't offer access to the middle of the trail. Taxis would need to be hired in order to get to and from Refugio El Pilar and Roque de los Muchachos. Bus services are available on the final descent, at the Mirador El Time and at the end of the trail at Puerto de Tazacorte. Check the website for full details of services, www.transporteslapalma.com, or tel 922 411 924 or 922 414 441.

TOURIST INFORMATION

The main tourism website for La Palma is www.visitlapalma.es. Tourist information offices are located at the airport and at various locations on or near the GR131.

- Airport, tel 922 967 044
- Santa Cruz, tel 922 412 106
- Fuencaliente, tel 615 390 616
- Puerto de Tazacorte, tel 922 480 803

STAGE 27

Faro de Fuencaliente to Fuencaliente

Start	Faro de Fuencaliente
Finish	Fuencaliente (Los Canarios)
Distance	7km (4¼ miles)
Total ascent	710m (2330ft)
Time	2hr 30min
Terrain	Fairly easy paths and tracks climb barren slopes of rugged lava and loose ash, with occasional steep gradients.
Refreshments	Restaurant at Faro de Fuencaliente. Plenty of choice at Fuencaliente.
Transport	TILP buses 200 or 201 link Santa Cruz with Fuencaliente. TILP bus 203 runs from Fuencaliente down to Faro de Fuencaliente.
Accommodation	Limited choice in Fuencaliente.

This is no more than a morning or afternoon walk; a mere warm-up for the rigours of the days ahead. There is plenty to see around the Faro de Fuencaliente, with two lighthouses and a *salinas*, or salt works. The ascent is on bleak and barren lava flows, strewn with ash, where vegetation struggles. Two notable volcanoes, the Volcán Teneguía and Volcán de San Antonio, are passed on the way to Fuencaliente.

There are two **lighthouses** at Faro de Fuencaliente. The original basalt block construction (opened in 1903) was damaged by an earthquake in 1939 and the red and white lighthouse (opened in 1985) replaced it. The old lighthouse now serves as an interpretative centre. The nearby *salinas* are evaporation pools, where sea water becomes increasingly saline, so that salt crystals begin to form. Paths allow the area to be explored and further information is available in the restaurant.

The interesting salinas below the Faro de Fuencaliente

Cabbage-like lechugas somehow manage to thrive.

On a clear day, views reveal the islands of Tenerife, La Gomera and El Hierro.

The two lighthouses at **Faro de Fuencaliente** stand in a car park where there is also a bus shelter. The first signpost for the GR131 stands across a road, with a map-board just beyond. The path is much gentler underfoot than the nearby lava, but the loose, crunchy, dusty ash takes some getting used to. ◀ Lava steps lead up to a road and the path continues on the other side, climbing further and crossing the road again at a signpost. The next time you reach the road, the path runs alongside, then crosses it around 150m (490ft). The *malpaís* terrain is difficult for vegetation to colonise and even hardy *calcosa* bushes tend to be small and grow far apart. A solitary pine is severely stunted. ◀

The path climbs steadily and the black-ash slopes give way to ruddy-hued lava flows that would be really difficult to negotiate without a path. Keep left at junctions with other paths, until you reach a marker where there is an option to climb the very red and rugged **Volcán Teneguía**, which erupted as recently as 1971.

If you're not tempted to make a summit bid, turn right and the path becomes a stony track, then a broad dirt road. Simply keep straight ahead, rising gently and crossing the concrete water channel of Canal del Estalo.

218

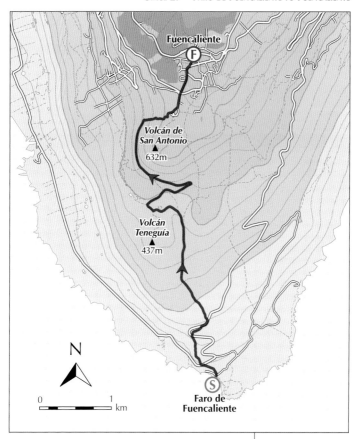

Reach a signposted junction of dirt roads beside a small vineyard, around 410m (1345ft), and turn left. There are good views from the slopes of **Volcán de San Antonio** as the dirt road rises gently around its flanks. ▸

There are a few pines on the slopes as well as a couple of information boards. Watch for a path signposted on the right, climbing and winding up a slope of pines and ash. When it reaches a road, there is

The end of the GR131, Puerto de Tazacorte, can be seen in the distance.

219

There is a visitor centre with an entry charge, tel 922 444 616.

the option of turning right to explore the **Volcán de San Antonio**, which erupted in 1677. ◀

Turn left up the road and go through a crossroads, climbing steeply up Calle Los Volcanes. Turn left at a higher road junction, passing the access road for the Bodegas Teneguía. Turn left up Calle Emilio Quintana Sánchez and continue straight up a brick-paved road to reach the main road through **Fuencaliente**.

FUENCALIENTE (LOS CANARIOS)

Technically, the district is known as Fuencaliente, having been named after hot springs that once existed. In recent years it was decided to refer to the village as Los Canarios, though not everyone agrees, and buses passing through might bear either name. There is a good range of services, including accommodation, bar-restaurants, shops, bank with ATM, buses and taxis. The villagers are grateful to the many walkers who pass through and support their economy. Look for the 'Hiker' sculpture near the church.

STAGE 28
Fuencaliente to Refugio El Pilar

Start	Fuencaliente (Los Canarios)
Finish	Refugio El Pilar
Distance	17.5km (10¾ miles)
Total ascent	1450m (4760ft)
Total descent	720m (2360ft)
Time	6hr
Terrain	Mostly clear paths and occasional tracks across slopes of ash or rock, forested or bare, with ascents and descents that are sometimes steep.
Refreshments	Plenty of choice in Fuencaliente. Possible snack van at Refugio El Pilar.
Transport	TILP buses 200 or 201 link Santa Cruz with Fuencaliente.
Accommodation	Limited choice in Fuencaliente; basic camping (advance permit required) at Refugio El Pilar.

This stage of the GR131 is a popular route in its own right, known as the Ruta de los Volcanes. As its name suggests, it passes several volcanic peaks, craters and lava flows, and some of them were formed in recent times. There are slopes of crunchy black ash, dense and sparse stands of pine and possibly some fine views. The Refugio El Pilar offers an opportunity to camp, but little else.

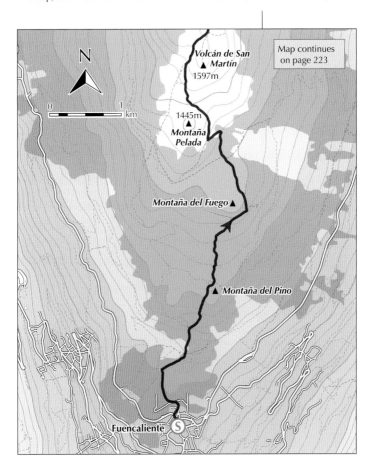

Start in **Fuencaliente** at a crossroads beside the Bar Parada, around 710m (2330ft). Walk along the main road as if heading towards Los Llanos, but turn right up the brick-paved Calle José Pons. Pass a statue of a hiker – *El Caminante* – near a church. A broad, stone-paved path climbs steeply, ending with steps where it crosses a road. More steps lead up a narrower path into pine forest that has obviously been burnt in the past.

Turn right along a road and right again when a path is signposted, which in turn leads through the forest to a track. Cross over it and follow a broad path a short way to where the GR130 crosses the GR131. ◄ Walk straight ahead up a rugged path and later cross a dirt road. The trees are dense but it should be possible to spot a mast on top of **Montaña del Pino**. The path crosses a track at around 1000m (3280ft), drops into a dip to cross another track, then climbs onwards.

There are signposts at path junctions on the slopes of **Montaña del Fuego**, but the GR131 is obvious anyway. After a gentler stretch, the route climbs in a steep zigzag on the slopes of **Montaña Pelada**. The pines thin out as the path crosses black ash, reaching a gap at 1382m (4534ft). The ascent continues and the colourful, red-flushed slope

The GR130 makes a complete circuit around La Palma.

A signposted junction on the way to Volcán de la Deseada

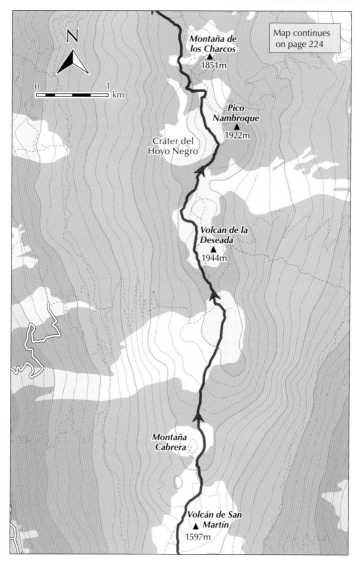

Map continues on page 224

223

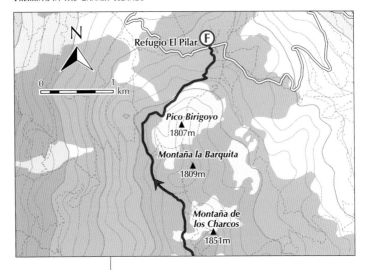

Refugio El Pilar ⒻⒻ

Pico Birigoyo
▲
1807m

Montaña la Barquita
▲
1809m

*Montaña de
los Charcos*
▲
1851m

The crater lies off-route, but contains a cave where there is a surprising steady drip-feed of water.

of **Volcán de San Martín** rises to the right. ◄ Walk along a ridge between craters, at 1557m (5108ft), and climb past pines onto **Montaña Cabrera**. There is a descent into a slight crater, then more climbing through forest, continuing up through a valley where the ash underfoot is loose. Eventually, cross a gap at 1861m (6106ft) and follow the path gently down to a signposted junction.

On the next gentle ascent, look out to the right, across the sea, to spot the distant peak of El Teide on Tenerife. A steep climb leads to the crater rim of **Volcán de la Deseada**. A trig point lies ahead at 1931m (6335ft), although it should be noted that the far side of the crater is a little higher, at 1944m (6378ft). Just before reaching the trig point, the marked path descends to the left. Bare ash, partially forested slopes and rugged lava flows are passed, then a short ascent leads to a ridge of lava overlooking a lava 'lake' and coal-black volcanoes.

The path climbs and passes through an area featuring quite stout pines. Leaving the forest abruptly, the path passes two big cairns near the edge of the awesome, deep, dark **Cráter del Hoyo Negro**, around 1880m

(6170ft). Descend and later swing left at a signposted junction. Go down into a forest and cross a footbridge. The path descends across the slope of **Montaña de los Charcos**, reaching an old track. Turn left to follow this down across the forested slopes of **Montaña la Barquita**.

Eventually, after some rugged stretches, turn right as signposted at a junction around 1610m (5280ft). A path climbs across a scree slope on **Pico Birigoyo**, touching 1650m (5415ft), then descends through tall pine forest where *tagasaste* bushes also grow. There are signposts and a map-board at **Refugio El Pilar**, around 1440m (4725ft).

REFUGIO EL PILAR

This is basically a large forest recreational area with picnic areas, barbecues, toilets, play equipment and car parking. Camping is allowed, so long as you obtain a permit. Organise this in advance, tel 922 423 100 extension 6820. Be warned that it can get cold and damp when mist drifts across the 'Cumbre', or just plain cold on clear nights. A mobile snack van might be parked near the road, but if the van isn't there then all food supplies need to be carried here. Water is always available. Despite there being a bus stop beside the road, there are no public bus services nearby. To leave the route you would need to call for a taxi pick-up.

Walking on an ash path through a valley near Montaña Cabrera

STAGE 29
Refugio El Pilar to Roque de los Muchachos

Start	Refugio El Pilar
Finish	Roque de los Muchachos
Distance	27km (16¾ miles)
Total ascent	1880m (6170ft)
Total descent	900m (2950ft)
Time	9hr
Terrain	Forest roads and paths give way to rugged mountain paths. Some ascents and descents can be steep.
Refreshments	None.
Transport	None. A taxi drop-off could be arranged at Refugio El Pilar, and a taxi pick-up could be arranged at the Roque de los Muchachos, but bear in mind that the highest part of the mountain road is closed each evening.
Accommodation	Camping at Refugio El Pilar (advance permit required), basic refuge at Punta de los Roques, none at Roque de los Muchachos.

This is a long and difficult stage, made more difficult because of the lack of easy access and lack of facilities along the way. After following the forested crest of the Cumbre Nueva, the trail climbs steeply through pine forest and traverses a succession of rocky peaks, finishing on the highest point on the island at the Roque de los Muchachos. Be sure to be well equipped up there; otherwise a pre-arranged taxi pick-up will be necessary.

Start on the roadside at **Refugio El Pilar** and walk up the road, through a cutting. Turn left onto a broad dirt road, but leave it almost immediately by following a path on the left, into dense laurisilva and pine forest. Keep left at a junction with another path. Join and follow the dirt road further along the Cumbre Nueva. ◄ After a long stretch on the dirt road, a short stretch of path is signposted to the left. The dirt road is crossed three times if all available paths are followed rather than

Note that the dirt road and the paths that run parallel are interchangeable. Feel free to use whichever appeals most.

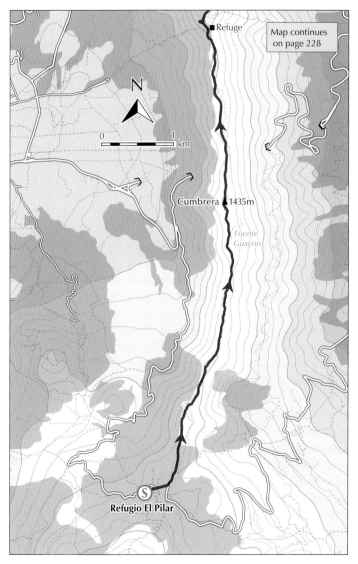

Refuge

Map continues on page 228

N

0   1 km

Cumbrera ▲1435m

Fuente Guayrin

S
Refugio El Pilar

walking on the road, then follow another long stretch of the dirt road, passing a signpost for **Fuente Guayrin**.

Tall masts rise above the forest on **Cumbrera**, at 1435m (4710ft), then another stretch of path is signposted on the left, up a few steps. This is much longer than the earlier stretches of path, and even when it gets

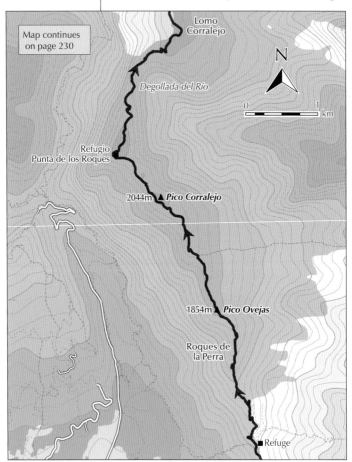

Map continues on page 230

Lomo Corralejo

Degollada del Río

N

0   1 km

Refugio Punta de los Roques

2044m ▲ *Pico Corralejo*

1854m ▲ *Pico Ovejas*

Roques de la Perra

■ Refuge

very close to the dirt road, marker posts and signposts keep pointing the way ahead. Eventually, a small stone building, a simple **refuge**, is passed just before you reach a path junction. Step up onto a track where there are signposts, as well as a small monument recording the opening of the GR131 and its incorporation into the trans-European E7 trail.

Follow the track uphill as signposted and switch to a path that starts with a few stone steps. The path joins the track at a higher level after avoiding a wide bend. The slope is mostly covered in pine forest, with an undergrowth of heather. Continue up the track, which gives way to a path, always climbing. The path is fairly well graded, zigzagging on the steeper slopes and never too rough underfoot. Pass a rocky outcrop as **Roques de la Perra**, continuing uphill to pass a signposted junction with another path. Further uphill, a signpost points left indicating a very short path to the summit of **Pico Ovejas**, at 1854m (6083ft). ▶

All other paths from here onwards drop to the right. There are no paths heading left into the precipitous Caldera de Taburiente.

Continue along a gentle pine-covered crest, where the path ahead is obvious. It passes a national park signpost where a notice points out that a rocky slope is part of **Pico Corralejo**, whose summit trig point can be spotted, at 2044m (6706ft). The path descends and passes beneath a cliff to reach a gap, then traverses beneath a peak, passing another cliff to reach another gap. The way ahead looks steep and difficult, but the path picks out the best line of ascent, suddenly reaching a shoulder on **Punta de los Roques**, where a refuge is available around 2050m (6725ft).

REFUGIO PUNTA DE LOS ROQUES

This basic refuge is available for passing trekkers, but all equipment, food and water needs to be carried there. Tables and benches are located in one small room, with sleeping platforms in another small room. Occasionally, there might be some stored rainwater collected from the roof, which might well need treating. Solar-powered lighting is available. There are often superb views of the Caldera de Taburiente and its surrounding mountains, sometimes seen across a 'sea of clouds'.

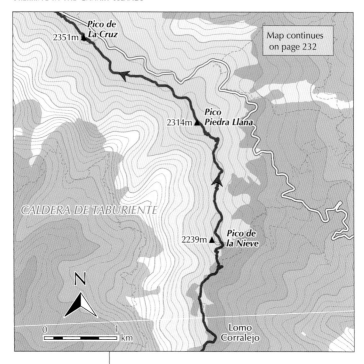

The awesome gulf of the **Caldera de Taburiente** was formed by a huge landslide, leaving tiered cliffs and steep, crumbling slopes in its wake. The area is a national park and the GR131 passes around its upper limits. There are no paths whatsoever that allow a descent into the caldera, but there are several splendid viewpoints looking down into it and across to the other side.

Follow the path onwards between two rocky peaks and start a fairly gentle descent. The path zigzags beneath tall cliffs where there is a danger of rock-fall. Cross the gap of **Degollada del Río**, at 1911m (6270ft), and soon afterwards pass a national park signpost. Pass another gap and climb along a crest, later passing a curious, bare, domed summit. Leave the forested crest and make a rising traverse across **Lomo Corralejo**. A path junction is reached among pines and broom. (If you would like to visit the Petroglifo Tagoror Pico La Sabina, carved by the original Auaritas of La Palma and protected by stout fencing, leave the main route by turning right here.)

The GR131 passes below the rock carvings, by which time access to them is barred by huge boulders. The path cuts across rocky slopes and crosses a gap, then climbs and passes a junction where there are national park signposts. The last pine trees are passed as the path climbs a slope of mixed scrub. It reaches a signpost at a junction where there are good views into the Caldera de Taburiente. Further along, another signpost points left for the nearby summit of **Pico de la Nieve**, at 2239m (7346ft).

The path crosses cliffs to reach the gap of Degollada del Río

The trail misses this summit and other summits ahead, always passing to the right of them while crossing scrub-covered slopes at fairly gentle gradients. Pass a sign for **Pico Piedra Llana**, close to its 2314m (7592ft) summit, followed later by a national park signpost. The path continues fairly easily, but later becomes rocky and boulder-strewn on the ascent of **Pico de la Cruz**. There is a concrete hut on the 2351m (7713ft) summit.

The path along the high mountain crest is never far from a road, and actually touches the road briefly at the **Mirador de los Andenes**, at 2283m (7490ft). The path climbs across a steep and crumbling slope and passes through a gap punched through the wall-like dyke of Pared de Roberto. Turn a prominent corner on the mountainside and descend to a gap at 2294m (7526ft). Climb past a huddle of strange observatories and reach a sign for **Pico Fuente Nueva**, at 2366m (7762ft).

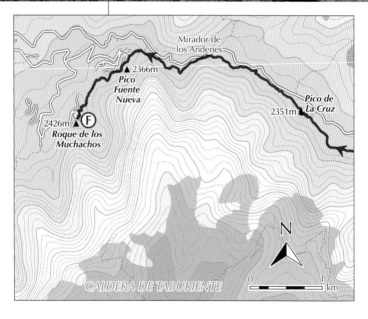

The cloud-filled Caldera de Taburiente
from Pico de la Nieve

Mirador de
los Andenes

▲ 2366m
Pico
Fuente
Nueva

Pico de
La Cruz
2351m

2426m ▲ Ⓕ
Roque de los
Muchachos

N

CALDERA DE TABURIENTE

0   1
└────────┘ km

Pass close to a road serving the observatories, climbing and descending again to reach a broad gap at 2326m (7631ft). ▶ A zigzag path finally leads up to a car park and a national park information hut on the **Roque de los Muchachos**. Although a trig point stands beside the car park, it is clear that a series of crumbling rock towers are slightly higher, around 2426m (7959ft), though these are surrounded by a fence to keep visitors from damaging them.

Look down to the right to spot ruined shepherd's huts.

ROQUE DE LOS MUCHACHOS

Although the summit is given as the end of this stage, and some trekkers will arrive equipped with their tents, food and water, it could take some time to locate a discreet place to camp. Please note that the observatories require dark skies and it would be unwise to go shining torches around at night (camping is not permitted and neither is light pollution). Trekkers who make arrangements to be collected and taken down from the summit not only need to arrive on time, but their vehicles must be off the summit road by 1800 and shouldn't return before 0700 the following morning. On the other hand, anyone with time to spare for further explorations should follow the stone-paved path from the summit down to spectacular viewpoints at Espigón, overlooking the Caldera de Taburiente.

The summit of Roque de los Muchachos

STAGE 30
Roque de los Muchachos to Puerto de Tazacorte

Start	Roque de los Muchachos
Finish	Puerto de Tazacorte
Distance	18km (11 miles)
Total ascent	100m (330ft)
Total descent	2520m (8270ft)
Time	5hr 30min
Terrain	Fairly easy mountain paths, occasionally steep and rugged, on both open and forested slopes. Assorted paths, tracks and roads at a lower level.
Refreshments	Bar-restaurant at Mirador El Time. Plenty of choice at Puerto de Tazacorte.
Transport	TILP bus 106 links Mirador El Time with Los Llanos. TILP bus 207 links Puerto de Tazacorte with Los Llanos, from where TILP bus 300 runs directly to Santa Cruz.
Accommodation	None at Roque de los Muchachos, but a good choice at Puerto de Tazacorte.

Enjoy views from Roque de los Muchachos before following fairly easy paths past other nearby summits. Apart from minor ascents, most of this stage runs downhill, first on open mountainsides, then through forest, then down cultivated slopes. The final part of the descent is an amazing zigzag path cut into a cliff, landing beside the sea at Puerto de Tazacorte.

Take every opportunity to enjoy paths leading to viewpoints near **Roque de los Muchachos** before leaving the summit for good. A path signposted as the GR131 runs downhill, joining the summit access road. Turn left and follow the road past a metal-clad building to reach a road bend. Turn left onto a track but immediately go down a path. This later rises and passes strangely shaped outcrops on **Roque Chico**, missing the 2371m (7779ft) summit.

Descend to a gap and climb a short way to a summit at 2318m (7605ft). The path continues and avoids the

The path climbs past the rocky peak of Roque Chico

next summit, skirting past it to cross a shoulder on Morro de la Crespa. Descend and eventually pass the gap of **Degollada de las Palomas**. The path crosses the slopes of **Roque Palmero** but keeps well below its summit, eventually passing a small pine tree. ▶ After passing a national park signpost there are enough pine trees growing for it to count as forested on **Pinos Gachos**.

The path descends past blocky boulders and some of the rock crumbles, releasing interesting dodecahedral crystals of garnet. There is a fine view into the **Caldera de Taburiente** from **Hoya del Estrabito**. The path descends across a slope that blocks views into the caldera for a considerable stretch, passing below the summit of **Somada Alta**, at 1925m (6315ft). Much later, walk along a rocky ridge and keep straight ahead at a national park signpost. Descend, then turn left to continue descending to a gap overlooking **Hoya Grande**, at 1344m (4409ft).

The path cuts across a slope and passes a hollow in the mountainside that has been planted with vines. A track leaves the hollow, but a path descends from it, passing another slope of vines. The path joins and follows a track, then yet another path continues downhill, crossing another

A fenced-off area contains rare specimens of bushy *Bencomia exstipulata*.

235

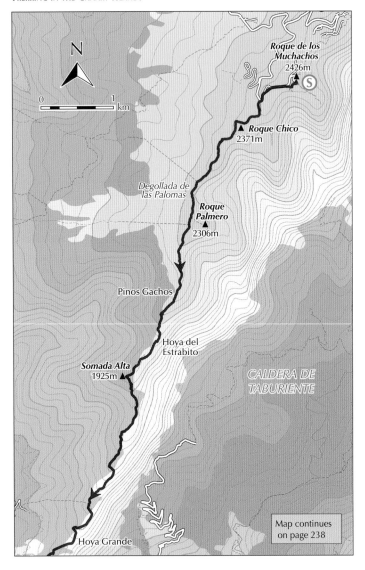

N

0   1 km

Roque de los Muchachos
2426m ▲ Ⓢ

▲ *Roque Chico*
2371m

Degollada de las Palomas

Roque Palmero
2306m

Pinos Gachos

Hoya del Estrabito

Somada Alta
1925m ▲

CALDERA DE TABURIENTE

Map continues on page 238

Hoya Grande

track. The descent is rather rugged underfoot, landing on a broader track where there is a signpost and map-board. Turn left to follow the track to a fire tower and viewpoint at **Torre del Time**, around 1170m (3840ft).

The track descends, becoming concrete, then take a broad and rugged path that drops from it. The surface can be knobbly rock, which is uncomfortable underfoot, or chunky boulder paving, but there are also short stretches of easier terrace paths. Continue downhill through pine forest, passing old cultivation terraces filled with tangled scrub, spotting a few houses at a lower level. A stone-paved ramp drops to a road at **La Pasada**, at 750m (2460ft).

Turn left along the road, then turn right along another path, as signposted. There are rugged and easy stretches on the way past the Casas de la Hacienda, then another road is crossed at **El Lomito**. The path rises gently, then descends past old scrub-filled terraces dominated by *tabaibal*. Cross a track at a derelict building to reach an edge at **Laderas de Amagar**. ▶ Walk down a rugged path with tangled water pipes alongside. Go through a path intersection where the GR131 crosses the GR130 – the latter encircling La Palma. The path later reaches a track,

A viewpoint at Torre del Time on the descent to El Time

Views stretch beyond Los Llanos to the Ruta de los Volcanes.

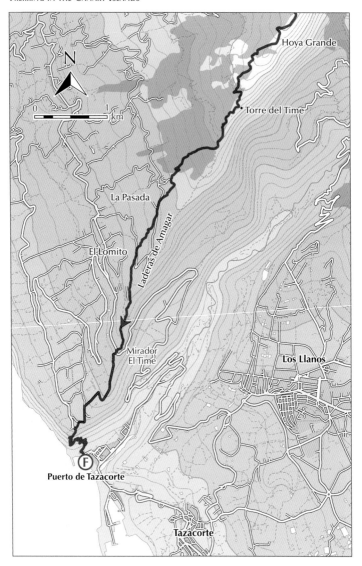

which becomes concrete, leading down to a road. Cross over and follow a short path behind a roadside barrier. There is access to the **Mirador El Time**, its bar-restaurant and bus services, around 510m (1675ft).

A steep road drops from the bar-restaurant down a scrub-covered slope, then it passes between tents where bananas are cultivated. Just before the tarmac ends, turn right to follow a track down across a slope of *tabaibal* and join another road. Continue descending between banana tents, turning left when signposted and later turning right round a bend. Watch on the left to spot a signpost. A concrete ramp and a stone-paved track drop to another road. Turn left and the road immediately gives way to a signposted, stone-paved path. This runs down alongside a cliff edge, then embarks on a steep, stone-paved, zigzag descent. Pass a few caves near the foot of the cliffs and quickly reach the final map-board and signpost between two bar-restaurants. Walk along the promenade at **Puerto de Tazacorte**, then turn left inland, and right to reach a prominent roundabout where there is a bus shelter.

Puerto de Tazacorte, at the end of the GR131 through La Palma

LA PALMA TO EL HIERRO

Getting from La Palma to El Hierro could be an awkward transfer, more so than transferring between any of the other islands so far. There is a large harbour at Puerto de Tazacorte and it would be wonderful if there was a ferry service direct to El Hierro, but unfortunately there isn't one. The distance between harbours is 100km (62 miles), but it is more than 265km (165 miles) using the available ferry services.

The transfer starts easily enough by catching TILP bus 207 from Puerto de Tazacorte to Los Llanos, changing to TILP bus 300 to reach Santa Cruz. The next step involves getting either the Fred Olsen or Naviera Armas ferry off the island, and the sailing could take place very early in the morning, though there are sailings in the middle of the day on Sundays. The Fred Olsen ferry takes 3hr to sail from La Palma to Los Cristianos on Tenerife, with a brief stop on La Gomera. The Naviera Armas ferry takes 4hr to complete the same journey, also with a brief stop on La Gomera.

The only ferry currently sailing to El Hierro is operated by Naviera Armas from Los Cristianos. Departure times vary and there might be days when there is no departure. The sailing generally takes 2hr 45min on a fast vessel. Be sure to check timetables well in advance and ensure that all the ferry services connect without undue delays.

If linking the ferry services together is going to cause problems or long delays, then it might be worth looking at flights instead. Flights from La Palma take only 30min to reach Tenerife Nord airport, from where a flight to El Hierro takes 40min. Flights are operated by Binter Canarias and the journey could be completed much more quickly than using the ferries, even if there is a sizeable gap between connecting flights.

Fred Olsen, tel 902 100 107 www.fredolsen.es

Naviera Armas, tel 902 456 500 www.navieraarmas.com

Binter Canarias, tel 902 391 392 www.bintercanarias.com

EL HIERRO

A flowery stretch of the Camino de La Virgen beyond San Andrés (Stage 31)

EL HIERRO
40km (25 miles) 2 days

The GR131 across El Hierro is based on a long-established pilgrim route across the high 'Cumbre', from a remote chapel to the main town of Valverde. The route is the Camino de La Virgen, and it attracts thousands of pilgrims in the middle of summer, every four years. The next pilgrimages, or Bajadas, will be in 2021, 2025, 2029, and so on. See www.bajadaelhierro.com for full details. The route of the pilgrimage has been extended at either end, allowing the GR131 to run coast to coast across the island.

There are two starting points. Trekkers arriving by ferry simply start walking from the ferry-port and follow a road and old paths up to Valverde. Those who arrive at the airport should take a short taxi ride to the coastal village of Tamaduste, where a slightly shorter alternative uses various paths, tracks and roads to reach Valverde. With both routes combined, the GR131 climbs steadily through farmland and forest, passing the village of San Andrés. A road junction at Fuente de La Llanía is roughly

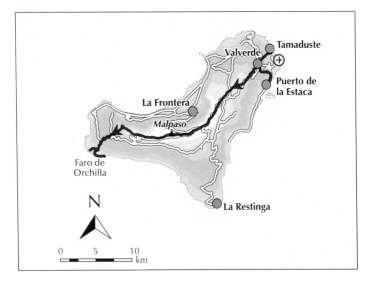

halfway along the route, but there are no services apart from a water supply.

The GR131 makes its way across slopes of crunchy black volcanic ash to reach Malpaso, which is the highest point on the island. A gradual descent from the bare ash slopes takes the route through forest and farmland to the remote chapel of Ermita de los Reyes. Rugged paths and roads are used on the way down arid slopes of scrub, ending in bleak surroundings at Orchilla. This was once quite literally the end of the world, and now it serves as the end of this long, island-hopping trail.

A good exit plan is needed, not only to get away from the end of the GR131, but also to get off the island, and eventually make your way home.

TRANSPORT

TransHierro buses serve the ferry-port, airport and the village of Tamaduste from Valverde, proving useful on the early stages of the GR131. Once beyond Valverde, the buses only reach as far along the GR131 as the village of San Andrés. The higher and western ends of the island are completely devoid of bus services. However, the island is small and TransHierro also operate taxi services, which will deliver trekkers to and from remote places such as Fuente de La Llanía, and will collect trekkers from the end of the GR131 at Orchilla. If relying on a taxi pick-up in a remote place, talk to a driver in advance, explaining exactly what you require and when they might expect your call.

Check the bus website for full details of services, www.transhierro.com, or tel 922 551 175. For taxis tel 922 550 729.

TOURIST INFORMATION

The tourism website for El Hierro is www.elhierro.travel. There are only two tourist information offices – a basic one at the airport (no phone; only staffed when flights arrive) and the main one in Valverde.

• Valverde, tel 922 550 326

STAGE 31

Puerto de la Estaca or Tamaduste
to Fuente de La Llanía

Start	Puerto de la Estaca or Tamaduste
Finish	Fuente de La Llanía
Distance	18km (11 miles)
Total ascent	1440m (4725ft)
Total descent	100m (330ft)
Time	5hr 30min
Terrain	Steep and rugged paths on the initial ascents, giving way to road-walking through town. Fairly easy tracks and paths usually climb at gentle gradients past farmland and forest onto the higher slopes.
Refreshments	Bar-restaurants at Puerto de la Estaca and Tamaduste. Plenty of choice at Valverde. Bar-restaurants off-route at San Andrés.
Transport	TransHierro bus 11 links Puerto de la Estaca with Valverde. TransHierro bus 10 links the airport with Valverde. TransHierro bus 6 links Tamaduste with Valverde. TransHierro bus 2 links San Andrés with Valverde. Call for a taxi if a pick-up is required at Fuente de La Llanía.
Accommodation	Limited choice in Tamaduste and Valverde but none at Puerto de la Estaca or Fuente de La Llanía: a pick-up may be necessary.

If you arrived by ferry, you can start walking straight from the ferry-port. Those arriving at the airport start walking from Tamaduste to Valverde, which is just 1km (½ mile) shorter than walking from Puerto de la Estaca to Valverde. The route continues climbing, passing the village of San Andrés, until a halt is called somewhere high and remote in the forested uplands.

Alternative route from Tamaduste

This route suits those who arrive at the airport. Simply get a short taxi ride to the nearby village of **Tamaduste** and ask to be dropped off as close as possible to the stone-paved promenade of Calle Río de Tamaduste. The cul-de-sacs of Camino Candil or Calle los Verodes lead onto the promenade. Go down steps onto a lower promenade and follow it past bathing places to reach the head of a cove surrounded by cliffs. Turn right to climb stone steps and walk a short way up Calle Los Tendederos to reach a map-board and signpost for the GR131. Another map-board and signpost are found at the end of the road.

Walk up a path that gives way to stone steps climbing to a road. Use a pedestrian crossing and go up more steps, turning left up a concrete path past a couple of houses. A stone-paved path continues uphill, winding past *tabaibal*, enjoying interesting views over Tamaduste and the airport. The path becomes more rugged as it climbs further but it also has some good stone-paved stretches. The path joins a black-ash track on **Lomo de Candía**, around 220m (720ft), where there are signposts and a small stone building. ▶

The steep, crumbling slopes of Montaña del Tesoro rise above the colourful buildings of Tamaduste.

Turn left and follow the ash track to a road bend. Turn right to follow the road uphill, which must be the steepest road on the entire GR131! Turn right at a road junction, as if approaching a house, but immediately switch to a path and climb over 50 log steps. The path continues climbing, and a steep slope of loose ash proves tiring on **Montaña del Hombre Muerto**, until over 100 log steps assist on the higher parts. The path joins a road and the road continues climbing more gently.

Turn right at a large building, a social centre, and turn left along a brick-paved road. Go straight through a crossroads, followed by another crossroads, to walk along Calle La Carrera. The road rises further into **Valverde**, passing through a signposted crossroads to follow Calle

Looking back to Tamaduste from the alternative route to Valverde

Doctor Gost. Pass the Hotel Boomerang to reach the Iglesia de La Concepción and a fine plaza. Climb over 50 stone steps as marked, turning right at the top to walk up Calle Pérez Galdós. Turn left along the stone-sett Calle Licenciado Bueno. At a signposted crossroads you join the GR131 main route from Puerto de la Estaca, around 590m (1935ft).

VALVERDE

This is the main town on El Hierro, situated inland and at some altitude. The name translates as 'green valley', and it is surrounded by cultivation terraces and plots. These contrast with the arid, scrub-covered lower slopes of the island, and the more forested uplands. Naturally, a full range of services is available and the town could be used as a base while walking the GR131, as there is no accommodation at all on the higher parts of the trail, but transport to and from the town is easily organised.

Main route from Puerto de la Estaca

This route suits those who arrive by ferry, but if the ferry arrives in the evening then it won't really be practical to start walking until the following morning. There is a bus service to and from Valverde and taxis usually meet the incoming ferry. Walk along the road away from the ferry-port at **Puerto de la Estaca**, quickly reaching a map-board and signpost. Turn right up the stone-paved Calle García Escamez, which zigzags up past houses and continues up a scrub-covered slope overlooking the harbour. Pass a solitary house just before joining a main road.

Turn right and follow the road uphill, later passing a small ruined building. Further along, there are two loops of abandoned stretches of road. Turn left along the second of these, then almost immediately turn left again as signposted to go up a rugged path on the slopes of **Pico de los Espárragos**. There is a good stretch of stone-paved path, then the surface is worn to uneven bedrock before reaching a signposted junction. Turn left to continue up the rugged path and there are later more stretches of stone paving. Signposts stand at the top of the path, near a road junction beside a sports centre in Valverde.

Use a nearby pedestrian crossing and watch carefully for red and white markers to walk along a backstreet as indicated by a notice reading 'Cash Alimentación'. There is a road junction and a pedestrian crossing at the end of the backstreet, then a flight of stone steps drop to a lower, stone-sett road. Turn left to follow this through the town centre, reaching a crossroads where there is a GR131 signpost. The alternative route from Tamaduste joins here, around 590m (1935ft).

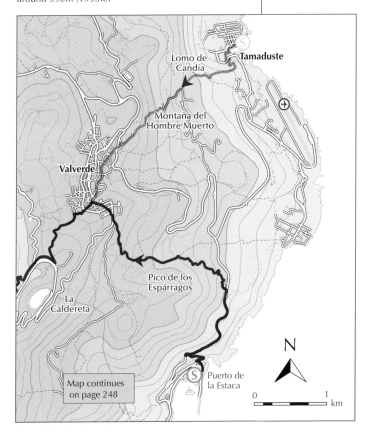

Puerto de la Estaca and the main route of the GR131 to Valverde

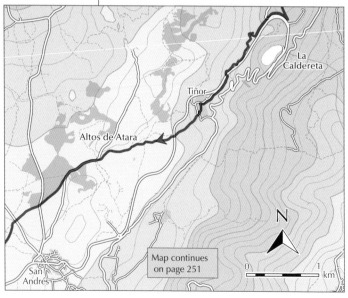

La Caldereta

Tiñor

Altos de Atara

San Andrés

Map continues on page 251

N

0   1 km

Turn left to walk up the street as signposted and the brick paving gives way to tarmac. Go through a tunnel beneath a higher road, reach a junction and turn left as signposted up Calle Fernández Armas. This climbs very steeply, but when it reaches a junction, turn left along the level Calle Casañas Frías. The tarmac gives way to a stone-paved track at some small caves and a notice about the 'Virgen' and the four-yearly pilgrimage. The track passes lush overgrown terraces and cypress trees as it climbs away from town.

Turn right along a minor road that runs parallel to a main road, reaching the cultivated hollow of Finca Quinta República at the head of a valley. ▸ Turn left up a narrow, grassy path and when the main road is reached again, turn right to walk parallel to it, behind a barrier fence. Turn right up a steep, stone-paved track, which becomes gravel, then stone-paved again, and later grassy. Look down to see a reservoir at **La Caldereta**.

The GR131 originally climbed straight uphill from the main road, but the route has been altered to avoid crossing it.

> **La Caldereta** was formerly an empty volcanic crater that was converted into a reservoir. At the same time **five wind turbines** were placed on a nearby crest. When the wind blows, the turbines generate electricity. Any surplus energy is used to pump water up into the reservoir. When the wind drops, the water is released, flowing down a pipeline to a hydro-electric power station on the coast. The balance between wind and water is enough to supply most of El Hierro's power requirements.

The track is narrow or broad, but always clear, eventually reaching the main road again. Cross to the other side to pick up and follow a narrow path running parallel to the main road, and a little below it. Reach a road junction and a bus shelter and turn left along the brick-paved Camino Central Tiñor, that leads to the scattered village of **Tiñor**. The *camino* becomes stone-paved later, climbing to a road that quickly terminates beside a small chapel, around 930m (3050ft). Climb another stone-paved track, the Camino Subida Tiñor, passing what is almost laurisilva forest, thriving on the moist air at this altitude.

Cross the main road and continue along the stone-paved track. Two junctions are reached close together near **Altos de Atara**, with the first one being signposted and the second one bearing a marker. Keep straight ahead at both, and the next couple of junctions are signposted as the track runs almost level through pine forest. Cross a road where there is a small picnic site, around 1030m (3380ft). ◄

Note that the village of San Andrés lies off-route to the left, offering bar-restaurants and occasional bus services.

Continue along a stone-paved track, passing fields and keeping straight ahead through an intersection of dirt roads. Keep straight ahead again at two junctions close together, and the track eventually crosses a road. Pass cypress trees and the track gives way to a stone-paved ascent, crossing the road again at a higher level near **Montaña de Afosa**. Rugged and delightfully grassy stretches of the track climb and cross the road yet again. Later, the track runs parallel to the road, passing a big pine tree near **Timbarombo**. Tracks off to the right quickly join the road, so avoid them and watch for markers to keep rising gently ahead.

Cross a crest at 1334m (4375ft), close to the road beside the hill called **Asomadas**, then descend a little and head towards a forest, crossing a grassy track. Watch for a path running closer to the road on the way through the forest, then cross the road as signposted and turn left to follow a black-ash track. The trees thin out and a signpost points to the right for the Mirador de Fireba. Follow the GR131 straight ahead and either pass close to a small viewing platform, or make a slight detour to include it, looking down into the crater of **Hoya de Fireba**. ◄

It is also possible to look across the sea and spot El Teide on distant Tenerife.

Continue following the path roughly parallel to the road, passing through laurisilva forest. Eventually, reach a parking space at **Fuente de La Llanía**, where water taps have been built into a wall. There are signposts, a map-board and a road junction, all around 1340m (4395ft). ◄

Unless you intend to camp discreetly or walk further along the trail, this is a good place to arrange a taxi pick-up.

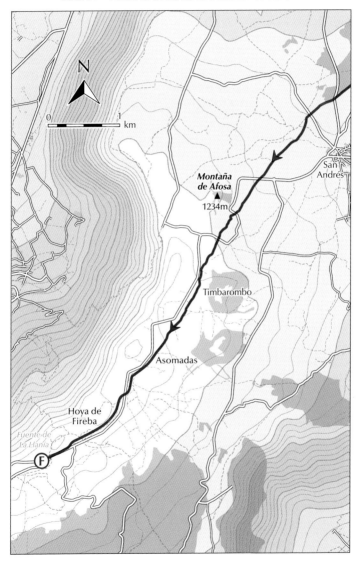

STAGE 32

Fuente de La Llanía to Embarcadero de Orchilla

Start	Fuente de La Llanía
Finish	Embarcadero de Orchilla
Distance	22km (14 miles)
Total ascent	240m (790ft)
Total descent	1580m (5185ft)
Time	7hr
Terrain	Fairly gentle tracks cross slopes of volcanic ash, becoming more rugged while descending through forest and farmland later. Roads and dirt roads become bendy towards the end but can be short-cut using rugged paths on barren slopes.
Refreshments	None.
Transport	None, though taxis can provide a drop-off and pick-up.
Accommodation	None at Fuente de La Llanía or at the end of the trail: you'll need to get a taxi to leave Embarcadero de Orchilla.

Map continues on page 255

The final stage of the island-hopping GR131 crosses Malpaso, the highest point on El Hierro, then gradually makes its way down to the remote Ermita de Los Reyes, passing through the barren landscape of La Dehesa to reach a very rugged coastline at Orchilla. This is a remote place to end a long walk, so either aim to be fully self-sufficient if spending a night out there, or have a good exit plan sorted in advance.

Start at the road junction at **Fuente de La Llanía**, surrounded by laurisilva forest, around 1340m (4395ft). Follow the road signposted for the Ermita Virgen de los Reyes, which is almost level. ▸ Pass a paragliding launch site and the two little rocks known as **Dos Hermanas**. Turn right as signposted along an ash track among trees. The track turns left and climbs from the trees, passing only a few isolated heather trees on a steep slope of pumice. ▸ Enjoy views over bare and forested slopes then come down through a stand of pines to reach a gap at Raya El Cépon, at 1358m (4455ft).

If the air is clear it should be possible to spot the distant island of La Palma.

La Gomera and El Teide come into view.

Climb across another crunchy slope and descend past a few pines to reach **Cruz de Los Reyes**. The nearby road changes from tarmac to a broad dirt road. Watch for signposts, backed up by red and white markers while passing junctions with other dirt roads. Pass a map-board in a dip, then the GR131 climbs steadily. Clip a couple of bends on a tarmac road, then watch for a broad, cairned path rising to the right. This reaches the top of **Malpaso**, where there is a stout pillar commemorating both the GR131 and the trans-European E7. Head a short way to the right to visit the summit trig point at 1501m (4925ft), beside a tall mast. ▸

A viewpoint also overlooks El Golfo, which was the scene of a massive landslide about 15,000 years ago when half of the island fell into the sea, possibly raising a huge tsunami.

Be sure to continue from the stout pillar, following a crunchy path flanked by stones. A track runs gently down across a fairly bare slope, reaching sparse pine trees where there is a signposted junction. Keep walking ahead, soon reaching another path junction for the remote village of Sabinosa. Continue downhill on the undulating track to reach a notice reading 'Punto de Encuentro El Pinar – Sabinosa'. A short stretch of the track is flanked by walls, and there is a glimpse down to the

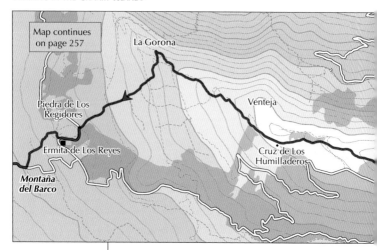

Faro de Orchilla, far below, from near **Raya de Binto**, around 1420m (4660ft).

A little further down a steeper slope, the tiny trickle of Fuente de Binto is fed when mist is caught by heather trees and drips into the ground. The track runs through a small forest of mixed laurisilva and pines; lots of lumber has been stacked on a bare slope beyond. A rocky slope of heather around 1300m (4265ft) gives way to a planted laurisilva forest. Keep straight ahead where another track crosses, following a grassy track, and the next junction bears a signpost. Leave the forest and soon pass **Cruz de Los Humilladeros**, where there might be water available from a tap.

As the track continues its descent is becomes very bendy, but some of the bends can be short-cut. Keep left at a junction to avoid one bend, dropping below 1250m (4100ft) and reaching a gate flanked by pines. Go through and continue down the track, keeping left at three more junctions as marked. Another junction has signposts, then there are more signposts at **La Gorona**, as well as a view over a steep edge around 950m (3115ft).

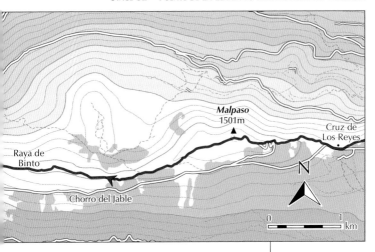

The track now descends much more abruptly past lush, grassy, flowery fields surrounded by fences, drystone walls or both. Always go straight downhill at junctions and note the increasing number of dense, hunched juniper bushes. Go down through a gate to reach a complex junction where a cubic block of rock sits at **Piedra de Los Regidores**, at 718m (2355ft). Turn left and follow a clear dirt road, which becomes a tarmac road leading down to the white-painted **Ermita de Los Reyes**, around 700m (2295ft).

> The little chapel of **Ermita de Los Reyes** contains a statue of the Virgin, which is said to have arrived on the island in 1546 and was originally kept in the nearby cave of Cueva del Caracol, until the first chapel was built in 1577. The statue was first carried across the island to Valverde in 1740, in the hope that this would alleviate a devastating drought. It rained copiously afterwards, so the islanders vowed to repeat the pilgrimage every four years. Their route became known as the Camino de La Virgen and it forms the backbone of the GR131 on El Hierro.

The *ermita* lies to the left of the road, while the GR131 turns right along a track, quickly reaching a cave, the Cueva del Caracol. Look carefully to find the only narrow, stony path running down a scrub-covered slope. Follow this path down to a road on the slopes of **Montaña del Barco** and turn right to cross a cattle grid, around 600m (1970ft). The road becomes very bendy on the slopes of **Montaña del Gamonal**, but resist the urge to short-cut.

Watch for a marker post on the left, around 480m (1575ft), where the first opportunity to short-cut is available. Even so, take care to follow the path marked by red and white paint marks, stones and cairns. Land on the road and turn left, then watch for stone and log steps leading downhill on the right. Cross the road again and continue down the path, from a rugged slope onto a slope of crunchy ash. Land on the road, turn left and follow it a short way, then turn right down another path. Cross the road again and quickly re-join it. Follow it onwards round a bend, reaching a signposted junction with a track.

Detour to Meridiano Cero 3km (2 miles) there and back, 90m (295ft) descent/ascent, 1hr

The original Zero Meridian was at the edge of El Hierro, which, until Christopher Columbus discovered the

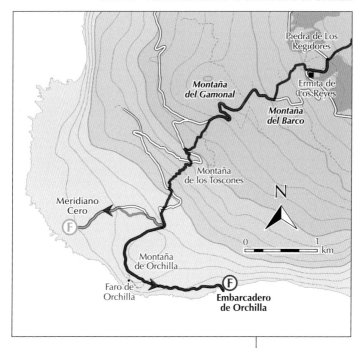

Americas, was thought to be the westernmost edge of the world. The GR131 includes an option to visit a small monument commemorating the meridian, but anyone going that way must return afterwards. Start by following a track as signposted, but watch for a red and white paint marker in order to switch to a streambed of ash and bare rock. Later, re-join the track and turn left to reach the monument. Retrace steps to the road and turn right to continue. ▶

The author has camped beside the monument, which is an option worth considering.

The road continues and a lighthouse comes into view. This is the **Faro de Orchilla**, around 110m (360ft). A short dirt road leads to it, but have a look at what is posted at the junction. One notice says that this is the end of the GR131, while a signpost insists that you should continue onwards. The road winds gradually downhill and eventually reaches a stout stone jetty at the **Embarcadero de Orchilla**. There is a picnic site and water might be available, otherwise this is the end of the road, and the end of the trek along the GR131 that started a long time ago and a long way away at Órzola on Lanzarote. If you walked all the way, then congratulations!

The end of the GR131

GETTING AWAY FROM THE GR131

There might be changes around the end of the GR131 in future. A plan has been put forward to convert the lighthouse into a small hotel. So, you will either finish at the end of a road with no accommodation, or possibly finish near a rather convenient hotel. Either way, this is a remote place on a remote island, a long way from home. An exit plan is required.

Taxis can be summoned to Orchilla and rather surprisingly they could appear in less than an hour. There are two options: either get a taxi to La Frontera and continue on TransHierro bus 3 to Valverde, or simply get the taxi all the way to Valverde, which will usually cost double the price. A night's accommodation may be required in Valverde before transferring to the ferry-port on TransHierro bus 11 or airport on TransHierro bus 10 to leave El Hierro.

Plenty of timetables will need to be juggled. If the ferry operated by Naviera Armas, tel 902 456 500 www.navieraarmas.com, is used to get from El Hierro to Los Cristianos on Tenerife, then it is likely that the TITSA 711 bus will be needed to transfer from Los Cristianos to Tenerife Sur airport for a flight home. If flying from El Hierro to Tenerife with Binter Canarias, tel 902 391 392 www.bintercanarias.com, or Canaryfly, 928 018 500 www.canaryfly.es, the flight will land at Tenerife Nord airport. A bus transfer will be needed to reach Tenerife Sur airport for a flight home. It might be better to fly from El Hierro to Gran Canaria, then transfer to a flight home without having to leave the airport.

The important thing is to plan your return in advance, rather than trying to figure everything out at the last minute.

APPENDIX A
Language notes

Apart from a few place names derived from original Guanche words, most names appearing on maps are Spanish. Many words appear frequently and are usually descriptive of landforms or colours. The following list of common words helps to sort out what some of the places on maps or signposts mean.

Spanish	English
agua	water
alto/alta	high
arenas	sands
arroyo	stream
asomada	promontory
bahía	bay
bajo/baja	low
barranco	ravine
barranquillo	small ravine
blanco/blanca	white
boca	gap
cabeza	head
caldera	crater
calle	street
camino	path/track
cañada	gully
canal	watercourse
carretera	road
casa	house
caseta	small house/hut
colorado/colorada	coloured

Spanish	English
cruz	cross/crossroads
cueva	cave
cumbre	ridge/crest
de/de la/del	of the
degollada	col/gap/saddle
el/la/los/las	the
embalse	reservoir
era	threshing floor
ermita	chapel/shrine
estación de guaguas	bus station
fuente	fountain/spring
gordo/gorda	fat/giant
grande	big
guagua	bus
hoya	valley
ladera	slope
llano	plain
lomo	spur/ridge
montaña	mountain
morro	nose
negro/negra	black
nieve	snow
nuevo/nueva	new
parada	bus stop
paso	pass
pequeño/pequeña	small
pico	peak

Spanish	English
piedra	rock
pinar/pino	pine
playa	beach
plaza	town square
presa	small reservoir
puerto	port
punta	point
risco	cliff
rojo/roja	red
roque	rock
san/santo/santa	saint (male/female)
sendero	route/path
valle	valley

APPENDIX B
Useful contacts

Island Government
Gobierno de Canarias (Canary Islands): www.gobiernodecanarias.org

Lanzarote: www.cabildodelanzarote.com

Fuerteventura: www.cabildofuer.es

Gran Canaria: https://cabildo.grancanaria.com

Tenerife: www.tenerife.es

La Gomera: www.lagomera.es

La Palma: www.cabildodelapalma.es

El Hierro: www.elhierro.es

Tourism
Lanzarote: www.turismolanzarote.com

Fuerteventura: www.visitfuerteventura.es

Gran Canaria: www.grancanaria.com

Tenerife: www.webtenerife.com

La Gomera: www.lagomera.travel

La Palma: www.visitlapalma.es

El Hierro: www.elhierro.travel

Inter-island flights
Binter Canarias
tel 902 391 392
www.bintercanarias.com

Canaryfly
tel 928 018 500
www.canaryfly.es

Inter-island ferries
Fred Olsen (all islands except El Hierro)
tel 902 100 107
www.fredolsen.es

Naviera Armas (all islands)
tel 902 456 500
www.navieraarmas.com

Líneas Romero (Lanzarote–Fuerteventura)
tel 928 596 10
www.lineasromero.com

Lobos (Fuerteventura–Lobos)
tel 638 572 971 or 616 986 982
www.navieranortour.com

Bus services
Intercity Bus (Lanzarote)
tel 928 811 522
www.arrecifebus.com

Tiadhe (Fuerteventura)
tel 928 855 726
www.tiadhe.com

Global (Gran Canaria)
tel 928 939 316
www.guaguasglobal.com

TITSA (Tenerife)
tel 922 531 300
www.titsa.com

Transportes La Esperanza (Tenerife)
tel 922 548 080

Guaguagomera (La Gomera)
tel 922 141 101
www.guaguagomera.com

TILP (La Palma)
tel 922 411 924 or 922 414 441
www.tilp.es

TransHierro (El Hierro)
tel 922 551 175
www.transhierro.com

El Teide
Visitor Centre
tel 922 922 371

Summit permit www.reservasparquesnacionales.es and click 'Teide'

Refugio Altavista www.volcanoteide.com

NOTES

NOTES

DOWNLOAD THE ROUTES
IN GPX FORMAT

All the routes in this guide are available for download from:

www.cicerone.co.uk/765/GPX

as GPX files. You should be able to load them into most formats of mobile device, whether GPS or smartphone.

When you go to this link, you will be asked for your email address and where you purchased the guide, and have the option to subscribe to the Cicerone e-newsletter.

www.cicerone.co.uk

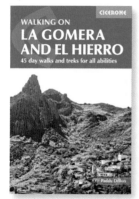

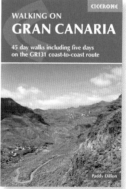

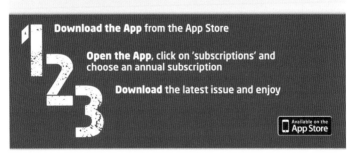

LISTING OF CICERONE GUIDES

SCOTLAND

Backpacker's Britain:
  Northern Scotland
Ben Nevis and Glen Coe
Cycle Touring in Northern Scotland
Cycling in the Hebrides
Great Mountain Days in Scotland
Mountain Biking in Southern and
  Central Scotland
Mountain Biking in West and North
  West Scotland
Not the West Highland Way
Scotland
Scotland's Best Small Mountains
Scotland's Mountain Ridges
The Ayrshire and Arran Coastal Paths
The Border Country
The Borders Abbeys Way
The Cape Wrath Trail
The Great Glen Way
The Great Glen Way Map Booklet
The Hebridean Way
The Hebrides
The Isle of Mull
The Isle of Skye
The Skye Trail
The Southern Upland Way
The Speyside Way
The Speyside Way Map Booklet
The West Highland Way
Walking Highland Perthshire
Walking in Scotland's Far North
Walking in the Angus Glens
Walking in the Cairngorms
Walking in the Ochils, Campsie Fells
  and Lomond Hills
Walking in the Pentland Hills
Walking in the Southern Uplands
Walking in Torridon
Walking Loch Lomond and
  the Trossachs
Walking on Arran
Walking on Harris and Lewis
Walking on Jura, Islay and Colonsay
Walking on Rum and the Small Isles
Walking on the Orkney and
  Shetland Isles
Walking on Uist and Barra
Walking the Corbetts
  Vol 1 South of the Great Glen
Walking the Corbetts
  Vol 2 North of the Great Glen
Walking the Galloway Hills
Walking the Munros Vol 1 – Southern,
  Central and Western Highlands
Walking the Munros Vol 2 – Northern
  Highlands and the Cairngorms
West Highland Way Map Booklet
Winter Climbs Ben Nevis and
  Glen Coe
Winter Climbs in the Cairngorms

NORTHERN ENGLAND TRAILS

Hadrian's Wall Path
Hadrian's Wall Path Map Booklet
Pennine Way Map Booklet
The Coast to Coast Map Booklet
The Coast to Coast Walk
The Dales Way
The Dales Way Map Booklet
The Pennine Way

LAKE DISTRICT

Cycling in the Lake District
Great Mountain Days in the
  Lake District
Lake District Winter Climbs
Lake District:
  High Level and Fell Walks
Lake District:
  Low Level and Lake Walks
Mountain Biking in the Lake District
Outdoor Adventures with Children –
  Lake District
Scrambles in the Lake District – North
Scrambles in the Lake District – South
Short Walks in Lakeland Book 2:
  North Lakeland
The Cumbria Way
The Southern Fells
Tour of the Lake District
Trail and Fell Running in the Lake
  District
Walking the Lake District Fells –
  Langdale
Walking the Lake District Fells –
  Wasdale

NORTH WEST ENGLAND AND
THE ISLE OF MAN

Cycling the Pennine Bridleway
Cycling the Way of the Roses
Isle of Man Coastal Path
The Lancashire Cycleway
The Lune Valley and Howgills
The Ribble Way
Walking in Cumbria's Eden Valley
Walking in Lancashire
Walking in the Forest of Bowland
  and Pendle
Walking on the Isle of Man
Walking on the West Pennine Moors
Walks in Ribble Country
Walks in Silverdale and Arnside

NORTH EAST ENGLAND,
YORKSHIRE DALES AND
PENNINES

Cycling in the Yorkshire Dales
Great Mountain Days in the Pennines
Mountain Biking in the
  Yorkshire Dales
South Pennine Walks

St Oswald's Way and St Cuthbert's
  Way
The Cleveland Way and the Yorkshire
  Wolds Way
The Cleveland Way Map Booklet
The North York Moors
The Reivers Way
The Teesdale Way
Trail and Fell Running in the
  Yorkshire Dales
Walking in County Durham
Walking in Northumberland
Walking in the North Pennines
Walking in the Yorkshire Dales:
  North and East
Walking in the Yorkshire Dales:
  South and West
Walks in the Yorkshire Dales

WALES AND WELSH BORDERS

Cycle Touring in Wales
Cycling Lon Las Cymru
Glyndwr's Way
Great Mountain Days in Snowdonia
Hillwalking in Shropshire
Hillwalking in Wales – Vol 1
Hillwalking in Wales – Vol 2
Mountain Walking in Snowdonia
Offa's Dyke Map Booklet
Offa's Dyke Path
Pembrokeshire Coast Path
  Map Booklet
Ridges of Snowdonia
Scrambles in Snowdonia
Snowdonia: Low-level and easy
  walks – North
The Cambrian Way
The Ceredigion and Snowdonia
  Coast Paths
The Pembrokeshire Coast Path
The Severn Way
The Snowdonia Way
The Wales Coast Path
The Wye Valley Walk
Walking in Carmarthenshire
Walking in Pembrokeshire
Walking in the Forest of Dean
Walking in the Wye Valley
Walking on the Brecon Beacons
Walking on the Gower
Walking the Shropshire Way

DERBYSHIRE, PEAK DISTRICT
AND MIDLANDS

Cycling in the Peak District
Dark Peak Walks
Scrambles in the Dark Peak
Walking in Derbyshire
White Peak Walks:
  The Northern Dales
White Peak Walks:
  The Southern Dales

SOUTHERN ENGLAND

20 Classic Sportive Rides in
South East England
20 Classic Sportive Rides in
South West England
Cycling in the Cotswolds
Mountain Biking on the North Downs
Mountain Biking on the South Downs
North Downs Way Map Booklet
South West Coast Path Map Booklet –
Vol 1: Minehead to St Ives
South West Coast Path Map Booklet –
Vol 2: St Ives to Plymouth
South West Coast Path Map Booklet –
Vol 3: Plymouth to Poole
Suffolk Coast and Heath Walks
The Cotswold Way
The Cotswold Way Map Booklet
The Great Stones Way
The Kennet and Avon Canal
The Lea Valley Walk
The North Downs Way
The Peddars Way and Norfolk
Coast path
The Pilgrims' Way
The Ridgeway Map Booklet
The Ridgeway National Trail
The South Downs Way
The South Downs Way Map Booklet
The South West Coast Path
The Thames Path
The Thames Path Map Booklet
The Two Moors Way
Two Moors Way Map Booklet
Walking Hampshire's Test Way
Walking in Cornwall
Walking in Essex
Walking in Kent
Walking in London
Walking in Norfolk
Walking in Sussex
Walking in the Chilterns
Walking in the Cotswolds
Walking in the Isles of Scilly
Walking in the New Forest
Walking in the North Wessex Downs
Walking in the Thames Valley
Walking on Dartmoor
Walking on Guernsey
Walking on Jersey
Walking on the Isle of Wight
Walking the Jurassic Coast
Walks in the South Downs
National Park

BRITISH ISLES CHALLENGES, COLLECTIONS AND ACTIVITIES

The Big Rounds
The Book of the Bivvy
The Book of the Bothy
The C2C Cycle Route
The End to End Cycle Route
The End to End Trail

The Mountains of England and Wales:
Vol 1 Wales
The Mountains of England and Wales:
Vol 2 England
The National Trails
The UK's County Tops
Three Peaks, Ten Tors

ALPS CROSS-BORDER ROUTES

100 Hut Walks in the Alps
Across the Eastern Alps: E5
Alpine Ski Mountaineering
Vol 1 – Western Alps
Alpine Ski Mountaineering
Vol 2 – Central and Eastern Alps
Chamonix to Zermatt
The Karnischer Hohenweg
The Tour of the Bernina
Tour of Mont Blanc
Tour of Monte Rosa
Tour of the Matterhorn
Trail Running – Chamonix and the
Mont Blanc region
Trekking in the Alps
Trekking in the Silvretta and
Ratikon Alps
Trekking Munich to Venice
Walking in the Alps

PYRENEES AND FRANCE/SPAIN CROSS-BORDER ROUTES

Shorter Treks in the Pyrenees
The GR10 Trail
The GR11 Trail
The Pyrenean Haute Route
The Pyrenees
Walks and Climbs in the Pyrenees

AUSTRIA

Innsbruck Mountain Adventures
The Adlerweg
Trekking in Austria's Hohe Tauern
Trekking in the Stubai Alps
Trekking in the Zillertal Alps
Walking in Austria

SWITZERLAND

Switzerland's Jura Crest Trail
The Swiss Alpine Pass Route –
Via Alpina Route 1
The Swiss Alps
Tour of the Jungfrau Region
Walking in the Bernese Oberland
Walking in the Engadine – Switzerland
Walking in the Valais

FRANCE

Chamonix Mountain Adventures
Cycle Touring in France
Cycling London to Paris
Cycling the Canal de la Garonne
Cycling the Canal du Midi
Écrins National Park

Mont Blanc Walks
Mountain Adventures in
the Maurienne
The GR20 Corsica
The GR5 Trail
The GR5 Trail – Vosges and Jura
The Grand Traverse of the
Massif Central
The Loire Cycle Route
The Moselle Cycle Route
The River Rhone Cycle Route
The Robert Louis Stevenson Trail
The Way of St James – Le Puy to the
Pyrenees
Tour of the Oisans: The GR54
Tour of the Queyras
Vanoise Ski Touring
Via Ferratas of the French Alps
Walking in Corsica
Walking in Provence – East
Walking in Provence – West
Walking in the Auvergne
Walking in the Brianconnais
Walking in the Cevennes
Walking in the Dordogne
Walking in the Haute Savoie: North
Walking in the Haute Savoie: South
Walks in the Cathar Region

GERMANY

Hiking and Cycling in the Black Forest
The Danube Cycleway Vol 1
The Rhine Cycle Route
The Westweg
Walking in the Bavarian Alps

ICELAND AND GREENLAND

Trekking in Greenland – The Arctic
Circle Trail
Walking and Trekking in Iceland

IRELAND

The Wild Atlantic Way and
Western Ireland

ITALY

Italy's Sibillini National Park
Shorter Walks in the Dolomites
Ski Touring and Snowshoeing in
the Dolomites
The Way of St Francis
Through the Italian Alps
Trekking in the Apennines
Trekking in the Dolomites
Via Ferratas of the
Italian Dolomites Vol 1
Via Ferratas of the
Italian Dolomites: Vol 2
Walking and Trekking in the
Gran Paradiso
Walking in Abruzzo
Walking in Italy's Cinque Terre
Walking in Italy's Stelvio
National Park

Walking in Sardinia
Walking in Sicily
Walking in the Dolomites
Walking in Tuscany
Walking in Umbria
Walking Lake Como and Maggiore
Walking Lake Garda and Iseo
Walking on the Amalfi Coast
Walks and Treks in the Maritime Alps

BELGIUM AND LUXEMBOURG
The GR5 Trail – Benelux and Lorraine
Walking in the Ardennes

**SCANDINAVIA:
NORWAY, SWEDEN, FINLAND**
Trekking the Kungsleden
Walking in Norway

**POLAND, SLOVAKIA,
ROMANIA, HUNGARY
AND BULGARIA**
The Danube Cycleway Vol 2
The High Tatras
The Mountains of Romania
Walking in Bulgaria's National Parks
Walking in Hungary

**SLOVENIA, CROATIA, SERBIA,
MONTENEGRO, ALBANIA
AND KOSOVO**
Mountain Biking in Slovenia
The Islands of Croatia
The Julian Alps of Slovenia
The Mountains of Montenegro
The Peaks of the Balkans Trail
The Slovene Mountain Trail
Walking in Slovenia: The Karavanke
Walks and Treks in Croatia

SPAIN
Camino de Santiago – Camino Frances
Coastal Walks in Andalucia
Cycle Touring in Spain
Cycling the Camino de Santiago
Mountain Walking in Mallorca
Mountain Walking in
    Southern Catalunya
Spain's Sendero Historico: The GR1
The Andalucian Coast to Coast Walk
The Camino del Norte and
    Camino Primitivo
The Camino Ingles and Ruta do Mar
The Mountains of Nerja
The Mountains of Ronda
    and Grazalema
The Northern Caminos
The Sierras of Extremadura
Trekking in Mallorca
Trekking in the Canary Islands
Walking and Trekking in the
    Sierra Nevada
Walking in Andalucia

Walking in Menorca
Walking in the Cordillera Cantabrica
Walking on Gran Canaria
Walking on La Gomera and El Hierro
Walking on La Palma
Walking on Lanzarote and
    Fuerteventura
Walking on Tenerife
Walking on the Costa Blanca
Walking the Camino dos Faros

PORTUGAL
Portugal's Rota Vicentina
The Camino Portugues
Walking in Portugal
Walking in the Algarve
Walking on Madeira
Walking on the Azores

GREECE
The High Mountains of Crete
Trekking in Greece
Walking and Trekking in Zagori
Walking and Trekking on Corfu

CYPRUS
Walking in Cyprus

MALTA
Walking on Malta

**INTERNATIONAL CHALLENGES,
COLLECTIONS AND ACTIVITIES**
Canyoning in the Alps
Europe's High Points
The Via Francigena Canterbury to
    Rome – Part 2

MOROCCO
Mountaineering in the Moroccan
    High Atlas
The High Atlas
Walks and Scrambles in the Moroccan
    Anti-Atlas

TANZANIA
Kilimanjaro

SOUTH AFRICA
Walking in the Drakensberg

TAJIKISTAN
Trekking in Tajikistan

JAPAN
Hiking and Trekking in the Japan Alps
    and Mount Fuji
Japan's Kumano Kodo Pilgrimage

JORDAN
Jordan – Walks, Treks, Caves, Climbs
    and Canyons
Treks and Climbs in Wadi Rum,
    Jordan

NEPAL
Annapurna
Everest: A Trekker's Guide
Trekking in the Himalaya

BHUTAN
Trekking in Bhutan

INDIA
Trekking in Ladakh

CHINA
The Mount Kailash Trek

**NORTH AMERICA:
USA AND CANADA**
The John Muir Trail
The Pacific Crest Trail

**SOUTH AMERICA:
ARGENTINA, CHILE AND PERU**
Aconcagua and the Southern Andes
Hiking and Biking Peru's Inca Trails
Torres del Paine

TECHNIQUES
Fastpacking
Geocaching in the UK
Lightweight Camping
Map and Compass
Outdoor Photography
Polar Exploration
Rock Climbing
Sport Climbing
The Mountain Hut Book

MINI GUIDES
Alpine Flowers
Avalanche!
Navigation
Pocket First Aid and Wilderness
    Medicine
Snow

MOUNTAIN LITERATURE
8000 metres
A Walk in the Clouds
Abode of the Gods
Fifty Years of Adventure
The Pennine Way – the Path,
    the People, the Journey
Unjustifiable Risk?

For full information on all our guides,
books and eBooks, visit our website:
www.cicerone.co.uk

Explore the world with Cicerone

walking • trekking • mountaineering • climbing • mountain biking • cycling • via ferratas • scrambling • trail running • skills and techniques

For over 50 years, Cicerone have built up an outstanding collection of nearly 400 guides, inspiring all sorts of amazing experiences.

www.cicerone.co.uk – where adventures begin

- Our **website** is a treasure-trove for every outdoor adventurer. You can buy books or read inspiring articles and trip reports, get technical advice, check for updates, and view videos, photographs and mapping for routes and treks.

- **Register this book** or any other Cicerone guide in your member's library on our website and you can choose to automatically access updates and GPX files for your books, if available.

- Our **fortnightly newsletters** will update you on new publications and articles and keep you informed of other news and events. You can also follow us on Facebook, Twitter and Instagram.

We hope you have enjoyed using this guidebook. If you have any comments you would like to share, please contact us using the form on our website or via email, so that we can provide the best experience for future customers.

CICERONE

Juniper House, Murley Moss Business Village, Oxenholme Road, Kendal LA9 7RL

✉ info@cicerone.co.uk   cicerone.co.uk